COOKING YOUR LOCAL PRODUCE

Cooking Your Local Produce

A COOKBOOK FOR TACKLING FARMERS MARKETS, CSA BOXES AND YOUR OWN BACKYARD

Greta Hardin

PHOTOGRAPHY BY VEE SAWYER

WARD STREET PRESS · SEATTLE · 2013

Cooking YourLocal Produce

info@wardstreetpress.com

If not available at your local bookstore, this book may be ordered directly from the publisher. For additional information about this book and about Ward Street Press, visit our web site at:

http://www.wardstreetpress.com

For additional information about Greta Hardin and *Cooking Your Local Produce*, visit Greta's web site at:

http://www.gretahardin.com

Cooking Your Local Produce

ISBN: 978-0-9887417-9-9
Editorial consultants: Elizabeth Budz-Falk & Kirk Wilson
Book & cover design by Vee Sawyer

AUTHOR ACKNOWLEDGMENTS ⎯⎯⎯⎯⎯⎯⎯⎯⎯⎯⎯⎯

I have many thanks to give, and they need to land all over. To my high school English teachers, at the Bush School, who taught me to write with my own voice, by helping me recognize the voices of others. To my Pomona College science professors who made the scientific method stick. To the early Colorado CSAs that stuck me with kale, kale, garlic and kale, thus making me do research. To The South 47 Farm for opening doors for me and my son. To Cindy Stinson for hiring me, and Nancy Carpenter, Robin Wyll, and Lucinda Brezak for a combination of support, suggestions, meetings, and some serious not interrupting. To Dog Mountain Farm the opportunity to stretch my teaching.

I also have to thank the Art Docents at Brookside for keeping me creative, and making me flex my brain. And most of all, Mary Christensen, you and your big ideas. How did I get so lucky? Thanks for bringing me together with John & Vee at Ward Street Press who have so patiently shepherded me through turning an idea all the way into a book.

And as I write this, I keep on thinking of all the little things and encounters that contributed, and keep thinking of things I've forgotten – and realize there's no way that I can name them all but get this in on time. Just know, that if you suspect you helped, you did, even if you just listened to me blather on and on about food, or did so in my presence. I also must thank all the people who heard the words, "Here, try this!" and did.

*To my parents who taught me
knives, fire, and the scout bite.*

*To my tasters:
Alec, for the right questions.
Tavin, for making it all new.*

contents

shoots 34

flowers 50

fruits   62

introduction

WHERE DO I BEGIN?

o to a farmers market and look around. Buy what tempts you. This is lots of fun and highly recommended, but when the produce gets home, the question is, "Now what do I do?"

Cooking Your Local Produce is all about answering that very question. This cookbook is a map that begins at "You Are Here." It was written to give you the knowledge and skills to cook with what you find, on the fly. It focuses on what you are most likely to pick up at a local farmers market or find looking up at you from a CSA bag or weekly veggie box. (CSA, or Community Supported Agriculture, are those local farms and organizations where you buy a share of the production up front. Once the harvest begins, each week you pick up and enjoy whatever is ready.)

If you didn't learn to cook at your grandmother's knee, or your uncle's ankle, or whatever, don't worry. *Cooking Your Local Produce* never requires prior kitchen knowledge or a particular variety of anything, like obscure salad greens, a specific pumpkin type, a precious vinegar, or a secret spice mixture. Instead the recipes, and the "resources" section on page 148, tell you everything you need to know. This book starts with the simple and familiar, and then shows the way to use produce you've never heard of or seen before. As you find your footing and get more comfortable asking questions and taste testing, use the recipes and the variations to expand the way you cook and the ingredients you use.

Never be afraid to substitute. After all, whoever figured out that roasting kale like a potato turned it into a crispy chip, was onto something. After getting a few cooking adventures (both rewarding and questionable), and some good meals under your belt, you will be ready to tackle any cooking challenge you choose.

BACKGROUND

This cookbook has its roots in a small pamphlet I developed for a "Farm-Tots" program where I was a teacher. Adults accompanied their small children around the farm. They touched, tasted, saw, and smelled produce growing from late spring into the early fall. While some of the parents were old hands at cooking with vita-greens, kohlrabi, and borage, most adults were just as curious as the kids about new varieties of produce, as well as the process of growing and picking the food.

Finding rainbow chard on red, white, pink, yellow, and green stems was exciting, but questions remained: What to do with chard when it came home? How to turn fresh produce into food that is as much fun to eat as it was to find?

I began by giving off-the-cuff suggestions, but the average adult juggling children, the days' pickings, the bag with a snack, and a dropped sandal couldn't absorb those ideas. They needed something they could look at later, when it was time to cook. I began my search for a cookbook that would give sound, simple advice for dealing with an enormous variety of fresh produce, without burying the reader in trivia or long lists of ingredients. I could not find a book to suggest. So I started on a pamphlet, and that grew into this book.

WHY ARE THE RECIPES WRITTEN THIS WAY?

My very oldest cookbooks have recipes that are barely two inches high, set in ten-point type. They were written by cooks for other cooks and read by people already familiar with cooking. *Cooking Your Local Produce* is for people ready to branch out into something new, so the recipes are written to explain new ingredients and techniques so even brand new cooks have all the information they need to make a successful dish.

The recipe pages in *Cooking Your Local Produce* are divided into the following sections:

INGREDIENTS. Look over this section to find a recipe that fits what you have, or to find out what you need to go out and get. If you aren't sure, check out the appendix (page 155) to see what I mean.

EQUIPMENT. I've included this section so you can get out everything you need at the start of the recipe, and never find yourself, like my father would, grumbling, "Wait, I need to find a grater, and a lid! Why didn't they say so earlier?" A short list of all the equipment you will need to cook anything in the book is included in the appendix (page 152).

PREP TOGETHER. Because nearly all the recipes begin with raw produce, there are often some steps that can be done hours earlier, or the night before, when there is more time. These are also perfect steps for teaching small children the basics of cooking, when you can go as slow as you need to. Raw produce can be left out on the counter for an hour or two, or wrapped loosely in the fridge. Cut fruit may be a little pickier, but most produce is hardy and not particular. That said, the prep work can also be done just before you cook. If some of the prep terms don't make sense, there are more complete descriptions in the appendix (page 148).

COOK! These are the steps that happen once you turn on the heat, and need to happen pretty quickly, or according to a timer. This is the point of no return, and once you start the cooking steps you usually need to keep going to the end. If some of the terms are unfamiliar, look them up in the appendix (page 148) for more explanation.

VARIATIONS. After cooking a recipe for awhile, you may want to make it taste a little different, or eat it with other dishes. At some point, "Ooooh! Chard!" may become, "eh, chard." Look to *Variations* to find ways to change up recipes and keep boredom at bay without having to learn a whole new recipe. A little change can make a familiar dish seem like a whole new thing.

SUBSTITUTIONS. You are planning on making your favorite squash recipe, but there are no delicatas in sight. Or maybe mustard greens and spinach showed up in the weekly veggie box, instead of the chard you expected. *Substitutions* is where you can look to see if the ingredients you have will work for the recipes you want to make. And don't be tied down by the things I mention. If what you have seems close enough to you, go for it.

Greta Hardin
Seattle, Washington
greta@gretahardin.com

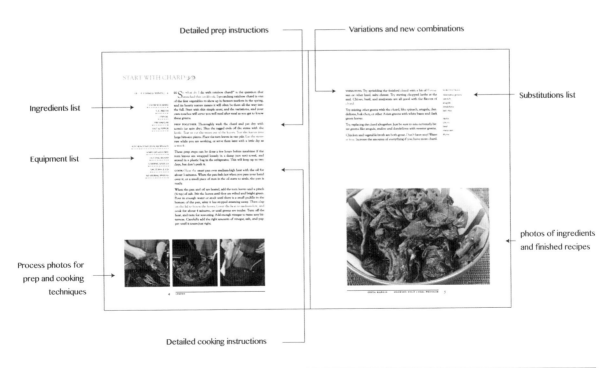

Detailed prep instructions — Variations and new combinations

Ingredients list →

Equipment list →

Process photos for prep and cooking techniques →

Substitutions list ←

photos of ingredients and finished recipes

Detailed cooking instructions

leaves

TENDER AND SWEET, HEARTY AND BITTER, & HERBS

When venturing into the world of local produce, the variety of greens is bewildering: light green, dark green, yellow-green, purplish-green, white-stripy green, and on and on. How do you know which ones are good for salad, and which are good for cooking, and if cooked, how to do it?

Start with a few big categories, the right questions, and a few simple recipes, instead of a long list of names, which are unstable as soon as you change regions.

All leaves can be placed into three main groups:

Tender and Sweet. These are good eaten raw, and are often mildly sweet: lettuces, frisée, cabbages, and "baby" anything fit this category.

Hearty and Bitter. These have strong flavors, sturdy textures and are often cooked before eating: chard, spinach, kale, vita-greens, endive, radicchio, arugula, collard, dandelion, and mustard greens are all hearty leaves.

Herbs. These are something pleasant by the leaf, but overwhelming by the mouthful, often used to add flavor to a whole dish by adding it at the beginning or as a last minute flourish: basil, oregano, mint, thyme, rosemary, parsley, dill, chives, cilantro, savory, marjoram, tarragon, and sage are all useful herbs.

Some leaves "boundary jump," like spinach, which is eaten raw and cooked, or cilantro (coriander leaf), which is used both as a salad green and as an accent.

When you venture into the farmers market, begin by asking what is tasty raw, and what is better cooked. Ask to try a bite. You immediately discover what that leaf is: sweet and watery, peppery, bitter, pungent, spiky, tough, or sour.

Staring into a CSA bag is the same. Nibble a little of each of the leaves to find out what sort of leaves you have. Then start deciding what needs to be done to each kind. The only observation that really matters is this: Would you like to eat it raw, would you prefer the taste and/or texture altered through cooking, or would it add a nice flavor to something else. How to enjoy your leaves raw and cooked is what this chapter is all about.

PURCHASING. Look for leaves that are crisp and sturdy, and have lively color. Stay away from anything too wilted, spotty, dry, brown, or slimy. Note that dirt is not a blemish; it rinses off easily, and is simply evidence that the produce was grown.

STORAGE. All leaves, when they arrive home, benefit from proper storage preparation. If left open or just in a plastic bag in the fridge, they have a one-to-three day shelf life. With a little preparation, this can extend out to a week or more, depending on the leaves.

EQUIPMENT. Kitchen towels (paper towels also work) and plastic produce bags (save the ones from the market or grocery store) are needed. A salad spinner is optional.

INSTRUCTIONS. Give all leaves a bath in a generous amount of water. Shake them off and either pat dry with the towels, or spin dry in a salad spinner. Get a kitchen towel damp, and squeeze out all excess water. Place the leaves in approximately a single layer (some overlap is fine), and loosely roll up the towels. Put the roll in a produce bag, twist the top shut, and store in your refrigerator where it won't get smashed. Now you have leaves instantly ready for at least a week.

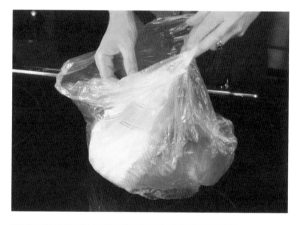

START WITH CHARD ❧

1LB = 1C COOKED SERVES 2 – 4

1 LB OR SO CHARD
....
½ C BROTH
....
1 TSP OIL
....
1 TBS VINEGAR
....
SALT & PEPPER
....

KITCHEN TOWELS/SALAD SPINNER
....
KNIFE
KID KNIFE–OPTIONAL
....
CUTTING BOARD
....
STIRRING SPATULA
....
SAUTÉ PAN & LID
....
MEASURING SPOONS
....

"So what do I do with rainbow chard?" is the question that launched this cookbook. Eye-catching rainbow chard is one of the first vegetables to show up in farmers markets in the spring, and its hearty nature means it will often be there all the way into the fall. Start with this simple sauté. The variations and your own touches will serve you well meal after meal as you get to know these greens.

PREP TOGETHER. Thoroughly wash the chard and pat dry with towels (or spin dry). Slice the ragged ends off the stems with the knife. Tear or cut the stems out of the leaves. Tear the leaves into large bite-size pieces. Place the torn leaves in one pile. Eat the stems raw while you are working, or serve them later with a little dip as a snack.

These prep steps can be done a few hours before mealtime if the torn leaves are wrapped loosely in a damp (not wet) towel, and stored in a plastic bag in the refrigerator. This will keep up to two days, but don't push it.

COOK! Heat the sauté pan over medium-high heat with the oil for about 3 minutes. When the pan feels hot when you pass your hand over it, or a small piece of stem in the oil starts to sizzle, the pan is ready.

When the pan and oil are heated, add the torn leaves and a pinch (¼ tsp) of salt. Stir the leaves until they are wilted and bright green. Pour in enough water or stock until there is a small puddle in the bottom of the pan, after it has stopped steaming away. Then clap on the lid to braise the leaves. Lower the heat to medium-low, and cook for about 4 minutes, or until greens are tender. Turn off the heat, and taste for seasoning. Add enough vinegar to tame any bitterness. Carefully add the right amounts of vinegar, salt, and pepper until it tastes just right.

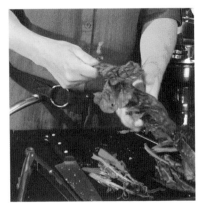  

VARIATIONS. Try sprinkling the finished chard with a bit of Parmesan or other hard, salty cheese. Try stirring chopped herbs at the end. Chives, basil, and marjoram are all good with the flavors of chard.

Try mixing other greens with the chard, like spinach, arugula, dandelions, bok-choy, or other Asian greens with white bases and dark green leaves.

Try replacing the chard altogether. Just be sure to mix extremely bitter greens like arugula, endive and dandelions with sweeter greens.

Chicken and vegetable broth are both great. Don't have any? Water is fine. Increase the amounts of everything if you have more chard.

SUBSTITUTIONS..

Alternative greens:
spinach
arugula
dandelions
bok choy

Herbs:
chives
basil
marjoram
thyme

CRISPY KALE

1 LB SERVES 2 – 4

KALE
....

OIL
......

SALT
....

CUTTING BOARD (OPTIONAL)
....

SHARP KNIFE (OPTIONAL)
....

KITCHEN TOWELS/SALAD SPINNER
....

BAKING SHEET
....

Make this recipe to try kale for the first time, or as a reintroduction after a bad kale experience. These "chips" are unexpected, tasty, and open to every variation you think of. Excellent with sandwiches. Kale's thick leaves and sturdy stems mean it can be grown year round, so these can be made anytime.

PREP TOGETHER.   Rinse the kale leaves well in plenty of water to remove dirt and any tiny residents. Pat dry with towels or spin dry. Tear the kale leaves from the tough stems by holding the stem in one hand and stripping the whole leaf off with the other. Cut or tear the leaves into hand-sized pieces.

COOK!   Heat the oven to 425°F. While the oven is warming up, toss the kale pieces on the baking sheet with a sprinkle of salt and enough oil to lightly coat the leaves (a tsp or so per large handful).

Bake in the oven until crispy. Check at 10 minutes. The total time can be anywhere from 10 to 25 minutes, depending on the type of kale and how much you have. Don't stack the leaves more than about 2 thick. Bake in multiple batches if there are lots of leaves.

VARIATIONS. Try sprinkling the leaves with different seasoning salts or lemon pepper. Try sprinkling on Worcestershire sauce at the beginning instead of salt for even more flavor. Try other thick leaves like collards, or mix in some mustard greens.

Kale is available in a range of colors and shapes and each variety sports several names. A dark green, smooth edged leaf with a pebbly texture is known as Black, Lacinato, and Tuscan kale.

Kales can have thin flat, pebbly textured, curly, thick, or waxy feeling leaves. They will vary in flavor and may have vastly different cooking times. Try the different kinds as you find them, and discover the best of your region.

SUBSTITUTIONS...

Greens:
collard greens
mustard greens

MODIFICATIONS...

season salt
lemon pepper
Worcestershire sauce
soy sauce

A BIG GREEN SALAD

SERVES 4

HALF A PRODUCE BAG OF LETTUCES
AND TENDER GREENS

2 TBS TASTY OLIVE OIL

1 TBS VINEGAR

1 TSP MUSTARD

1 CLOVE GARLIC

SMALL HANDFUL OF TENDER HERBS

PINCH OF SALT & PEPPER

CUTTING BOARD

SHARP KNIFE (KID KNIFE – OPTIONAL)

KITCHEN TOWELS/SALAD SPINNER

SALAD BOWL & SERVING UTENSILS

FORK/WHISK

MEASURING SPOONS

SUBSTITUTIONS...

Good salad herbs:
parsley, basil, chives, cilantro, dill

Nuts for salads, roughly chopped:
hazelnuts, pecans, walnuts, peanuts, almonds

When spring and summer lettuces are available, start your meal plans with a salad. Not sure what else to have? Make the salad as a base to the meal. Then you can think of something to go along side, or decide to add some protein to build the salad into a meal. If the salad is complete, and you are still stumped, make a quick omelet or a soft-boiled egg on toast. Ta Da! A sophisticated, satisfying meal.

PREP TOGETHER. Smash and peel the garlic clove. Chop the garlic and the herbs finely. Place these in the salad bowl. Add the vinegar, mustard, salt and pepper. Whisk in the oil. (Or, combine all the dressing ingredients in a small, tightly lidded container and shake them.) If there is too much dressing, store it in the fridge for the next salad. Wash the leaves thoroughly. They may even need two washes. Spin dry or pat dry with towels.

COOK! Chop or tear the leaves into bite size pieces. Toss with enough dressing to coat all the leaves, but not so much they are swimming in a puddle. Assemble the salad right before you serve it.

VARIATIONS. Try adding a few other items of in-season produce, and don't shy away from new combinations. See the *New Combinations* list on the following page for a few ideas.

Dressing options. This is a classic "vinaigrette" dressing made from a fat (the oil), an acid (the vinegar), and an emulsifier (the mustard). All of these basic ingredients can be replaced with another of the same category. Try changing your dressing as the ingredients change. Or add herbs that are in season with the greens you get.

Different acid. Try a different vinegar or citrus juices. The tarter flavors, like lime, work especially well when adding meats to salad, like bacon, steak, or chicken.

Other tasty oils. Try hazelnut, walnut, avocado, sesame, or peanut. These can be mixed with a neutral oil (one that has little to no flavor of its own) if they have a particularly strong flavor. Or use a neutral oil to let other salad flavors shine through.

Hazelnut oil dressings make the most of apples in salads. Walnut oil's hint of bitterness is welcome in salads with strawberries and other sweet fruits. Sesame oil's savory flavor compliments meats added to salads. Avocado oil adds richness to crunchy vegetables.

Emulsifiers. These are ingredients that allow oil and water (or water-based ingredients like vinegar) to mix for a while. Mustard is the classic, and any mustard works. Try your favorite, or something new, from the yellow ballpark stuff to a colorful seedy variety. Try some other tasty kitchen ingredients that emulsify like a smashed roasted garlic clove or a paste made by mincing anchovies.

Try substituting the garlic with thinly sliced onions, scallions, shallots, or in the spring, green garlic chutes or scapes. Try changing the herbs to suit other additions to the salad. Mint goes with apples or pea pods. Savory mixes well with green beans. Marjoram goes well with baby spinach. Parsley, dill and cilantro go with almost anything.

Some people swear by adding a little sweetness to their dressing. Try honey, or a pinch of sugar, or orange marmalade. A mildly sweet dressing can balance out bitter greens like frisée, arugula or endive.

Try a "hard salad" with very little or no lettuce at all. Use sprouts, roots (for example, carrots, jicama, beets) shoots, and cooked grains (rice, quinoa, cracked wheat, barley, kamut, or other cooked grains, and use the cooking directions on the container they come in.)

NEW COMBINATIONS...

spinach & strawberry
peach & purple onion
apple & nut
red pepper & sweet onion
bacon & melted leek & radish

GREEN GODDESS SALAD

SERVES 6 – 8

DRESSING:

¾ C MAYONNAISE

¼ C SOUR CREAM

2 TBS THINLY SLICED CHIVES

2 TBS THINLY SLICED FLAT LEAF/
ITALIAN PARSLEY

2 TSP CHOPPED TARRAGON

2 TBS (OR MORE) THINLY SLICED HERBS

1 TBS MINCED SHALLOTS

1 TBS LEMON JUICE

3 ANCHOVY FILLETS OR
1 TBS ANCHOVY PASTE

SALT AND PEPPER TO TASTE

A PRODUCE BAG FULL OF
TENDER SPRING GREENS

SHARP KNIFE (KID KNIFE – OPTIONAL)

CUTTING BOARD

LARGE SALAD BOWL & SERVING
UTENSILS

SMALL MIXING BOWL & SPOON

KITCHEN TOWELS/SALAD SPINNER

MEASURING CUPS & SPOONS

Make this salad to celebrate the arrival of fresh spring greens — tender, sweet, peppery, hints of bitter, and tangy-sour. Leafy herbs like parsley and cilantro add more excitement. The elaborate dressing makes it a salad worthy of special occasions. The herbs and leaves listed here are a starting point, feel free to experiment.

PREP TOGETHER. Thoroughly rinse the herbs and salad greens. Pat or spin the greens dry. Chop the herbs and onions. Chop the anchovy fillets finely and smash them into a paste.

Combine all the dressing ingredients except for salt and pepper, and stir well. Taste for seasoning and add salt and pepper until it tastes just right. This is a good place to stop, wrap and refrigerate the greens, and let the dressing rest in the fridge for a few hours to let the flavors blend.

COOK! Wash and tear (or cut) the greens. Dress the greens just before serving.

VARIATIONS. Try making just the dressing to use as a dip for fresh vegetables. Just reduce the mayonnaise to ½ C. Try using extra dressing over baked or roasted potatoes and other root vegetables. Try using the dressing in tuna or chicken salad as the "secret ingredient."

The stand out star in this salad is the tarragon in the dressing, and the complex support of the other fresh herbs. Please try using the real or "full-fat" versions of sour cream and mayonnaise for this recipe. The extra ingredients in low- and non-fat versions can dull the herbal flavors. When you get really good at this, whip up a batch of tarragon mayonnaise sometime.

SUBSTITUTIONS...

Herbs:
1 tsp of basil, dill, thyme, or cilantro

No shallots? Try:
spring onions
green onions
scallions
regular onion

Greens:
lettuces, sorrel, baby kales, or baby spinach

HEARTY GREENS (FOR GRILLED FOOD) ❧

8 OZ = 1.5C COOKED, SERVES 2 – 4

0.5 – 1 LB HEARTY GREENS

1 SMALL ONION

2 TSP OIL

1 TBS VINEGAR

½ C BROTH

SALT & PEPPER

½ TBS BUTTER (OPTIONAL)

CUTTING BOARD

SHARP KNIFE (KID KNIFE – OPTIONAL)

SAUTÉ PAN & LID

STIRRING SPATULA

KITCHEN TOWELS/SALAD SPINNER

MEASURING SPOONS

When stumped for a quick vegetable make hearty greens. The numerous variations make it a match for whatever else is coming to the table. It brings dark greens back and leaves bland and bitter flavors behind.

PREP TOGETHER. Thoroughly rinse the greens and pat or spin them sort-of dry (damp is fine for this recipe). If the greens have thick, fibrous stems, tear the leaves from the tough stems by holding the stem in one hand and stripping the whole leaf off with the other.

Ignore thin, tender stems. Roughly chop or tear the leaves into pieces approximately the size of your palm. Cut the onion or shallot in half through the root end. Peel off any dry outer layers, and slice thinly.

COOK! Put the oil in the pan, and place it over medium high heat for 3 or 4 minutes. Put a small piece of onion in the pan; when it sizzles, the oil is ready. Add the onion with a pinch of salt. Stir the onion until it begins to turn translucent. Add a large handful of leaves; stir until they wilt. Continue to add the leaves this way until they all fit into the pan.

Once all the leaves are in, pour in the water or stock (more for more leaves, less for less). Lower the heat to medium and clap on the lid for 10 minutes. After that, check the greens to see if they are tender. If not, simmer with the lid on for a few more minutes. Add another ¼ C of liquid if the pan is dry.

When they are tender, add the vinegar to tame any bitterness. Cook for another minute or two with the lid off to evaporate some of the liquid. Taste for salt and pepper, add any if necessary. If you are feeling fancy, right before serving, stir the butter into the greens to give them a silky finish.

VARIATIONS. Try adding a few bitter or spicy greens in the mix to create interesting flavors (don't worry, the bitter mellows to a savory flavor with cooking). Some bitter greens to try are dandelion, frisée, endive, and radicchio. Spicy greens include American or Japanese mustard greens, mizuna, and radish greens.

Try an Asian variation. Substitute soy sauce for salt and sesame oil for butter.

Try the "I Don't Like Onions" variation. Substitute 1 or 2 smashed, peeled, and chopped garlic cloves for the onion.

Try adding bacon if you're feeling like a Southern variation. Cut a slice of bacon into thin pieces. Add the bacon when you add the oil. Cook it until crisp. Remove it from the pan before adding the onion, then cook the greens the same way. Add the crisp bacon bits back in at the end.

Try some Indian flavors. Use a purple onion. Add 1 tsp whole cumin seed and a ¼ tsp of ground coriander when you add the onion. If you have a ripe tomato, chop that up and stir it in too.

If you like a little heat, chop up a hot pepper (serrano, jalapeño, etc.) and add with the onions.

SUBSTITUTIONS...

Greens:
kale, any variety
collards
chard
spinach
cabbage
bok-choy
tatsoi

And mix in:
mustard
mizuna
arugula
dandelions

Broth:
Chicken and vegetable are good
Don't have any broth? Water works too.

Try some Thai flavors. Add 2 smashed, peeled, and chopped garlic cloves to the onions, along with a tsp of curry powder, ¼ tsp ground coriander and ¼ tsp ground cumin. At the end of cooking, stir in ¼ C or more of coconut milk.

If you like a little heat, chop up a hot pepper (serrano, jalapeño etc.) and add with the onions.

Try Middle Eastern flavors. Add 4 smashed, peeled, and chopped garlic cloves to the onions. Use purple onions if you have them. Stir in 1 large, or some smaller chopped tomatoes right before you add the leaves. Dress the cooked leaves with lemon juice instead of vinegar. If you have it, stir in a spoonful of tahini at the end.

Try creamed greens (of creamed spinach fame). Cut the greens smaller — about finger width pieces. When the greens are cooked to tenderness, add 3 Tbs butter, let it melt. Then sprinkle on a tablespoon of flour, and stir it in thoroughly. Add ½ C milk, cream, or chicken broth. Cook 5 minutes until the sauce starts to thicken. Check for flavor, and add any salt, pepper, or nutmeg for the classic French cuisine touch.

If you want to completely transform these greens, run the creamed greens through the blender to create a rather fancy purée, which can then be thinned with chicken or vegetable stock and made into soup. (Okay, I'll stop now.)

◀▲ Some hearty greens you have to buy, but several types come to you as bonus freebies! When you purchase fresh turnips, beets, radishes, carrots (yes, really) the greens on top can be washed and cooked this way too — quickly when they're small, longer when they're big.

BRAISED GREENS WITH SPICY SAUSAGE

8 OZ = 1.5 C COOKED SERVES 3 – 5

0.5 - 1 LBS MIXED HEARTY GREENS
....
4 PRE-COOKED SAUSAGES
....
SALT & PEPPER TO TASTE
....
½ C BROTH
....
1 ONION
....
1 TBS OIL
....

CUTTING BOARD
....
SHARP KNIFE (KID KNIFE – OPTIONAL)
....
SOUP POT, DUTCH OVEN, OR OTHER
HEAVY LIDDED POT
....
KITCHEN TOWELS/SALAD SPINNER
....
FORK
....
MEASURING CUP
....
MEASURING SPOONS
....

This takes the place of salad on wet or cold days. Start making this while figuring out what else to have for dinner. If you are still stumped when this is ready, just add some rice, small pasta, roasted potatoes, or garlic bread for a tasty, warming, satisfying meal.

PREP TOGETHER. Thoroughly wash the leaves, pat or spin dry. If the greens have thick, fibrous stems, tear the leaves from the tough stems by holding the stem in one hand and stripping the whole leaf off with the other. Roughly chop or tear the leaves into pieces approximately the size of your palm. Cut the onion in half through the stem end, pull off any outer dry layers. Slice the onion thinly.

COOK! Place the pot over medium high heat. What you do next depends on whether the sausages are raw or precooked. Add 1 Tbs of oil to the pot, and heat for 3 or 4 minutes. Brown the sausages and set aside. Lower the heat to medium, add the onion to the pot. Cook until the onion starts to become translucent. Add the chopped leaves and the stock, stir to combine with the onions or garlic and cover with the lid for 15 minutes.

While the greens are cooking, slice the sausage into your favorite size. After 15 minutes, check the greens. If they are approaching tender, add the sausages slices for about 10 more minutes of cooking. If the greens are still tough, keep cooking until they are almost tender (try another 10 minutes), then add the sausage. Add salt and pepper if they are needed.

When the greens are tender and the sausage is hot, enjoy!

VARIATIONS. Try with garlic instead (or add garlic as well). Use 3 to 5 cloves of garlic. Smash, peel, and chop the garlic. Add it where the onion would go, and cook until it just starts to take on some color. Then continue as before.

Try with uncooked sausage (there may be something spectacular at your farmers market). Prick the sausages well with a fork, and place them in the pot as it heats. Turn them occasionally to brown on all sides. You can check for doneness by cutting one. When thoroughly cooked all the way through, set the sausages aside. Keep at least 1 Tbs of the fat and juices that cooked out of the sausages in the pot. Then continue with the recipe as before.

This is a very forgiving recipe and can expand or contract to suit your needs. Leftovers emerge from the fridge sound and tasty for several days.

SUBSTITUTIONS...

Greens:
kale
mustard
beet
turnip
cabbage
collards
spinach
chard
dandelion

Sausages:
Italian (sweet or hot)
chicken apple
lamb & garlic
Andouille

The cooking method used here, "sauté then braise" or cooking over high heat with onions or garlic and some salt, adding a little liquid and then covering and steaming until tender, is a method that works with just about any vegetable. Beans, broccoli, squash chunks, cauliflower, carrots; if you have it, you can try it. There are three important things to do: 1) add flavor and/or seasoning during the sauté part, 2) test the vegetable about every 5 minutes while it is braising so you can find "done," 3) check the flavor of the vegetable at the end of braising, and add any salt, pepper or vinegar it needs. ▼

GREEN RICE

SIDE DISH FOR 4 – 6

1 C SPINACH

1 TBS BUTTER OR OIL

2 C MEDIUM GRAIN WHITE RICE

4 C WATER

1 TSP SALT

CUTTING BOARD

SHARP KNIFE

2 QT SAUCEPAN WITH A LID
(OR RICE MAKER)

MEASURING CUPS

MEASURING SPOONS

KITCHEN TOWELS/SALAD SPINNER

Make this when you want to have rice, and, ummm, something else. Mint and parsley for lamb; a little rosemary and lots of chives with pork; oregano, marjoram and arugula with something and tomatoes. Add basil and spinach for rice that goes with darn near everything.

PREP TOGETHER.   In a large amount of water, thoroughly wash the greens, and pat or spin dry. If the leaves have a large fibrous stem, tear or cut the leaves off the stems. Stack the leaves, roll them to give you control of the stack, and slice them into thin strips (chiffonade).

COOK!   Place the saucepan over medium high heat and add the butter. After 3 or 4 minutes, when the pan is hot, add the sliced greens and the salt. Stir until they are wilted. Add the rice, stir the greens in. Pour in all the water. Bring it all to a boil, reduce to a simmer, and cover. Simmer until all the water is absorbed (about 20 minutes). When the rice is finished, turn off the heat, give it one more stir, cover it back up, and let it steam until dinner is ready.

VARIATIONS.   Chop up half an onion, and add it in with the greens. Try using other grains (quinoa, barley, emmer, fahkir, amaranth) or couscous (tiny traditional or large Israeli). Just follow the instructions on the package, or follow this rule of thumb, err, pinky:

Grains generally will cook fine if you place them in a medium saucepan and add water until it covers the grain plus 1 inch (that's just over the top joint of your pinky). Bring the whole thing to a boil, then cover and simmer for 20 minutes. If the water is not absorbed at that point, and the grain is still tough or too chewy, simmer for 10 minutes more. If still not done, check every 5 to 10 minutes. And don't worry if there is water left over, just drain it off. That beats burned grains every time.

Try stirring in two handfuls of grated Parmesan cheese, ¼ C of chicken stock or cream, and a cup of fresh shelled (or frozen) peas just as the rice finishes. Clap the lid back on for 10 more minutes to melt the cheese and gently cook the peas off the heat. This is a very simplified version of the Italian gem *risi e bisi* (rice and peas). Offer salt and pepper at the table with this one.

Try using brown rice (directions will call for a bit more water and a longer cooking time) for a heartier flavor. Try using a handful of herbs instead of, or along with the greens.

Rice cooked with flavorings is found throughout the rice eating world: Asia (North, South, and Central), the Middle East, and all around the Mediterranean Sea. The practice has been enthusiastically adopted in South and Central America (cilantro-lime rice anyone?). Join the party and add some spice to your rice.

SUBSTITUTIONS...

Any rice works. Use your favorite, or try a new one.

Greens:
arugula
mustard greens
a few Tbs of any fresh herb
a few tsp of any dried herb

COMBINATIONS...

parsley & garlic & mint
basil & oregano & marjoram
arugula & garlic & tomato
red onion & 1 tsp cumin seed
cabbage & garlic & 1 tsp caraway seed
cilantro & lime (add these at the end of cooking)

HERBS GO EVERYWHERE

*Not so much a recipe, but a way to see herbs...
and some reasons to, maybe, start growing a few.*

So you have a recipe calling for 2 Tbs of chopped something: basil, rosemary, thyme, whatever. But you had to buy an entire herb packet, or bunch, and it just sits in the refrigerator, looking up at you every time you open the door, slowly rotting. I have done this countless times. One day, I realized, I didn't need a recipe to use up that last half-a-handful of herbs. They could go anywhere.

Omelets are an exceptional place to start. Soon soups, cheese sandwiches, and salads all beckon. Simply add in the handful of what you have. Unless it is rosemary. Or sage. These tougher, heartier herbs, in their raw states, have particularly strong, resiny flavors and can overwhelm a dish.

The first time you use too much sage is most likely close to the time you recognize a difference between tender-leaf herbs and hearty herbs. Tender-leaf herbs are those fragile creatures often used fresh, at the end of recipes, and are almost useless in their dried state. Hearty herbs, on the other hand, are most often cooked in a dish, and are usually no fun to chomp on alone. They also tend to be useful in their dried state.

Like all the other categories in this book, there are plenty of fence straddlers. Dried parsley is just green confetti, but it is good added at the beginning or the end of cooking. Dill and mint dry beautifully, are pleasant added at either the start or finish end of the cooking process, and are enjoyable raw in a salad. Don't worry, there is no definitive list. Deciding which herbs are tender and which are hearty is completely up to you and your taste buds.

Once you start adding herbs to salads, mixing them into dressings, slipping them in sandwiches, and making up herb oils to go over everything, you might decide it would be nice to grow your own. After all they don't take much work, or water, or space. Besides, those little $2.98 plastic packets add up fast and go bad quickly. The chives on your deck, railing or counter are always fresh, as long as you remember to keep them watered.

All you need to get started is one pot of chives. Give it a little water every few days, a view out a window, and a pat now and then. One day, it will bloom. This was my first edible flower, and it can also be yours. Enjoy it plain, maybe with a loved one, or save it for yourself. Pop off the spiky globe of lavender buds, and individually eat the separate flowers. Note the floral oniony taste, and the tiny hint of sweetness at the base of each tiny bloom.

It took me a while to start using my herbs on a regular basis. My first pots of herbs sat there on the deck, feeling lonely, much like the old packets in the fridge. Like any new habit, it took an effort to get it to stick. Now, I enjoy being an herb gardener, and it is easy to share with my son. The small scale of the operation is just right. And the herbs don't mind getting nibbled on, in fact, they thrive on it. And he still enjoys the novelty and bragging rights of consuming that first chive flower each spring.

HERB SIMPLE SYRUPS

Bring 1 C water and 1 C sugar to a boil. Pour it over 1 tightly packed cup of herbs (basil, thyme, mint — use less for rosemary and lavender). Let it cool. Strain into a clean container with a tight-fitting lid. Keep in the fridge and use to flavor seltzer water, lemonade, ice tea, and other drinks.

BASIC BASIL PESTO

MAKES ABOUT 1.5 C
(USE ¼ C ON PASTA FOR 2)

2 C BASIL LEAVES

½ C TASTY OLIVE OIL

¼ C PINE NUTS

2 OZ. PARMESAN CHEESE (¾ C GRATED)

1 CLOVE GARLIC

SALT & PEPPER TO TASTE

CUTTING BOARD

SHARP KNIFE

BLENDER

KITCHEN TOWELS/SALAD SPINNER

SMALL SHALLOW PAN

MEASURING CUPS

MEASURING SPOONS

Make pesto the first time you have a leftover handful of basil. Realize that if nothing else, you now have time to figure out what to do with it, instead of watching the leaves slowly turn that odd gray color. Then try it on a cracker, or a mushroom, or a tomato. I know! Why didn't I try this sooner? Now, experiment with other herbs.

PREP TOGETHER. In a large amount of water, thoroughly rinse the basil leaves and pat or spin dry. Pluck the leaves off the stems.

COOK! Heat the oven to 350°F. In a shallow pan, toast the nuts for 5 or 6 minutes. (Keep an eye on them, they burn in the blink of an eye.) Set aside and let cool. Place the Parmesan and garlic into your food crusher of choice. Pulse until the mixture has been turned into tiny pieces. Add the basil, nuts, and half of the olive oil. Pulse to combine. Alternate adding a little olive oil and pulsing until the mixture is smooth. Taste for seasoning; add salt and pepper as needed.

Use some right away, tossing it with freshly boiled pasta or gnocchi. Smooth the rest over, and cover with a thin layer of oil. Store this in a tightly lidded container in the refrigerator for a few days, or in the freezer for a few months.

VARIATIONS.   Try creating other herb pestos (pesto is simply Italian for "paste," so this is allowed).

Parsley and mint pesto. 2:1 parsley:mint, and add some lemon zest. Feta cheese instead of Parmesan gives it a Greek twist.

Tarragon and hazelnut pesto. Replace ¼ to ⅓ of the basil with tarragon, and use hazelnuts instead. This is amazing on chicken and white-fleshed fish.

Try small batches. ½ C of leaves, a Tbs of nuts, part of a garlic clove, 2 Tbs of cheese and 2 Tbs of oil makes a small experimental batch for trying new ideas. Try replacing the olive oil with nut oils.

Your homemade pesto is the perfect topping for that farmers market pasta you've been eying. Cook the pasta according to the directions you got at the stall (or are on the package). Stir the pesto into the hot pasta. Serve with some fresh veggies you've cooked using "sauté and braise" (see page 17) and you've got a complete meal.

Toss with warm pasta or rice. Add some to minestrone soup, transforming the Italian classic in to the French Provençal version, *Soupe de Pistou.* Spread it on toast, or on one side of a sandwich. Spread it on fish or chicken before baking. Try tomato, pesto, and mozzarella cheese for an excellent salad or sandwich. Toss it with roasted summer squash or potatoes.

SUBSTITUTIONS...

Other food crushers that are good at making pesto:
food processor
mortar & pestle

Nuts:
walnuts
hazelnuts
pecans

Oils:
walnut oil
hazelnut oil
pistachio oil

ARUGULA PESTO &
WHOLE WHEAT PASTA

MAKES ABOUT 1.5 C
USE ¼ C ON PASTA FOR 2

1 C ARUGULA

1 C SPINACH

2 OZ. PARMESAN CHEESE (¾ C GRATED)

2 – 3 CLOVES GARLIC

¾ C SALTED & ROASTED PISTACHIO NUTS

1 LARGE TOMATO

$^1/_3$ C TASTY OLIVE OIL

8 OZ. WHOLE WHEAT PASTA

CUTTING BOARD

SHARP KNIFE

MEASURING CUPS

MEASURING SPOONS

BLENDER

KITCHEN TOWELS/SALAD SPINNER

SOUP POT + LID

COLANDER

LONG SPOON

SERVING BOWL + SERVERS

At the height of its growing season, arugula's strong flavor and bitter bite can stampede a home. Make this to save some of the summer sharpness for dark winter. Or as a way to have a fast pasta side dish at your finger tips any time of year.

PREP TOGETHER.   Place the soup pot $^2/_3$ full of water over high heat to bring it to a boil. In a large amount of water, thoroughly rinse the arugula and pat or spin dry. Cut the core and stem out of the center of the tomato. Cut it into quarters, and use your fingers to remove the seeds and the gel stuff that goes with them.

COOK!   Place the Parmesan cheese and garlic into the food crusher of choice. Pulse to turn the mixture into tiny pieces. Add the arugula, nuts, tomato, and half of the olive oil. Pulse to combine. Add a little olive oil and pulse. Continue alternately adding olive oil and pulsing until the mixture is smooth. Taste for seasoning; add salt and pepper as needed.

When the water finally reaches a boil, drop in the pasta for 7 to 9 minutes. (Check a noodle at 7 minutes. If it's too crunchy, wait a few more minutes.) When the pasta tastes ready, pour into the colander. Immediately place the drained pasta in the serving bowl and stir in large spoonfuls of the pesto.

Keep adding pesto until the noodles are well sauced. Smooth over the remaining pesto in a container, cover with a thin layer of oil. Store this in a tightly lidded container in the refrigerator for a few days, or in the freezer for a few months.

VARIATIONS. Try mixing other leaves or herbs with arugula. Spinach and parsley are excellent additions. Try other grains with the pesto – bulgur wheat (tabbouleh), couscous, rice (brown or white). Cook according to the directions on the package, or use the pinky rule (see Green Rice on page 18).

Try tossing with lentils or other beans, and maybe a little more garlic. Legumes can be stubbornly bland. Try this pesto as a sandwich spread, or simply a pesto and cheese sandwich (toasting is an excellent addition). Try adding to tuna or chicken salad as a secret ingredient.

Always taste your arugula before making this pesto. Arugula that is more bitter than peppery needs to be cooked. Make sure the arugula used for this is peppery, barely sweet, and only a little bitter.

SUBSTITUTIONS...

Some other food crushers that are good at making pesto:
food processor
mortar & pestle

Other leaves to mix with the spinach:
basil
pea shoots
cilantro

GREMOLATA

Pesto's less oily, zingier cousin. It was traditionally an accompaniment to fried dishes. In our modern, border-crossing food world, go ahead and use it as a topping for meats, fish, strongly flavored vegetables as well. Or add a variation to cooked grains (bulgur wheat, couscous, quinoa, barley, etc.) for a dish that gives a thankful nod to tabbouleh.

PREP TOGETHER. Pull the parsley leaves off the large central stems. Chop the leaves until they are in tiny confetti sized pieces. Stop chopping before you end up with parsley juice.

COOK! Carefully grate, or peel and finely chop the bright yellow part of a lemon peel from ½ a lemon. Smash, peel, and finely chop the garlic clove. Combine all the ingredients.

VARIATIONS. Try adding about a Tbs of finely chopped nuts — almonds, hazelnut, pine nuts, walnuts, or pecans. Try other citrus fruits — oranges, tangerines, limes. Try different or a mixture of herbs — mint, oregano, basil, rosemary, thyme. Try adding a little juice from the citrus fruit you used.

Some possible combinations to consider:

Parsley/mint. Gremolata with lemon and almonds over grilled chicken.

Parsley/thyme. Gremolata with orange and hazelnuts over grilled trout.

Parsley/basil. Gremolata with lemon and pine nuts over grilled salmon or fried cod.

Parsley/cilantro. Gremolata with lime with fajitas.

Work with what you have to make the next great thing!

Try as a topping with simply grilled meats to add to a cookout. Try gremolata with fish and shellfish, especially when you add the citrus juice to the mixture. Try gremolata as a topping for strongly flavored vegetables like broccoli, kale or asparagus. Try using gremolata to add vibrant color and flavor to simple steamed cauliflower.

Try along side any breaded food, baked or fried. You can serve up the classiest fish sticks. It adds life to anything with breadcrumbs. This will liven up meatloaf or meatballs of any stripe.

HERB OILS

Begin by using herb oils for dipping bread. Then start drizzling them over vegetables, egg dishes, and then your main dish. Herb oils can also add depth and delicious mystery to you home-made salad dressings. Pretty soon you will be the master of pulling that little something out of your fridge to make the meal so much better.

PREP TOGETHER. Wash and dry the herbs and pull the leaves off the big stems.

COOK! Place the herbs in the blender. Add half the oil and pulse briefly. Stop the blender, pushing any whole leaves down into the chopped oil and leaves. Add the rest of the oil, put the lid back on, and run the blender until the oil and herbs are smooth and well combined. If you have time, let it sit for 10 to 20 minutes, and taste to see if it needs salt or other seasoning. Add carefully and stir until it tastes just right.

VARIATIONS. Begin with single flavor oils like basil, rosemary, thyme, cilantro, garlic scape, and chive. Then try creating your own combinations. Experiment by using oils that have their own flavors: olive oils, nut oils, add garlic, onion, fresh hot peppers, or red pepper flakes. Try this oil in salad dressings, or as a way to herbal flavors to meats and soups. Try mixed with pasta or rice. Try in grain salads or over grilled vegetables.

Use herb oils within a week of making them, and store in the refrigerator. Oils lack the water to allow biological bad guys to grow (mold, bacteria, spores, etc.) but juicy herbs bring some in. Herb oils you buy in the store have been made safe through pasteurization, but that is beyond the scope of this book. As long as you refrigerate your oils and use them within a week, you will be well inside the safety zone.

FLATBREAD

MAKES 6 – 8 PIECES

1 C WARM WATER

2 TSP YEAST

1 TBS HONEY/SUGAR

1 TSP SALT

3 ½ C FLOUR

A LITTLE OIL

EXTRA FLOUR FOR KNEADING
AND ROLLING OUT

MEASURING CUPS

MEASURING SPOONS

SMALL BOWL

LARGE BOWL

PLASTIC BAG

FLIPPING SPATULA

SAUTÉ PAN/GRIDDLE

I know, you probably aren't getting flour at the farmers market. But as far as I'm concerned, people who know how to make their own bread, even if they don't do it all the time, make the world a better place. And if you've never made yourself any bread, start with this one. It is a tiny investment of time, and trying again is easy. And the raw dough is fun to taste and play with.

PREP TOGETHER. In 1 cup of warm water (about 100°F — bathing temperature), stir in the honey, and then sprinkle on the yeast. Let it get foamy. In the mixing bowl, stir together the salt and flour. With clean hands, make a small well in the center of the flour, and pour in the foamy, yeasty water. Use clean hands to begin stirring the flour into the liquid. Be prepared to add up to another ½ cup of flour. Keep stirring and combining the flour and water until you have a smooth unsticky dough. Turn the dough out on a clean surface, sprinkled with flour. Knead the dough until it is stretchy. Roll it into a ball.

Pour a little oil into the plastic bag. Put the kneaded dough in the bag, and coat the outside of the dough ball with the oil. Place the dough in the bag in a warm place to rise for an hour or two — until it has doubled. After rising, punch down the dough, and turn it out onto a floury surface. Knead it some more, until it regains the smooth, stretchy texture. Divide into 6 or 8 equal pieces, and flatten each one into a roughly circular shape, about ¼-inch thick.

COOK!   Heat a sauté pan over medium heat (or a griddle to medium). Spread a little oil on the pan (griddle) and place the bread on it for 4 to 6 minutes, until the heated side begins to look a little browned. Flip the bread, and keep it on the heat until the bread is cooked through and has a bit of crunchy browning. Enjoy as warm as you can!

VARIATIONS.   When it is time to let the dough rise, you can wrap it up in its bag, and put it in the refrigerator for up to a week. When you are ready for bread during the week, simply take the bag out, and let it rise in a warm spot until it has doubled in size (about 2 hours). Continue with the recipe when you punch the dough back down.

You can also take out only part of the dough, and let it rise in a bowl, with a damp towel or plastic wrap over the top of the bowl (this keeps the dough from drying out) and continue with the recipe.

FLATBREAD WITH HERB OIL & LEFTOVERS

MAKES 6 – 8 PIECES

FLAT BREAD
....

HERB OIL
....

SUGGESTIONS:
leftover cooked vegetables
tomato and sweet onion slices
other lonely leftovers
salt & pepper
grated or sliced cheese

YOUR REFRIGERATOR
....

SHARP KNIFE
....

CUTTING BOARD
....

BOX GRATER (OPTIONAL)
....

SUBSTITUTIONS...

Don't have flatbread?
Tortillas & pita bread work fine too.

Transform the perennially despised leftover into something that looks suspiciously like pizza. Check your fridge today for the necessary ingredients. Sliced chicken, the end of a piece of cheese, herbs from the garden and that last zucchini are starting to sound really good all of a sudden.

PREP TOGETHER. Pull all the likely looking leftovers out of your refrigerator. Assemble your favorite combinations either on a whole flatbread or broken up to bite size servings. Make notes, so you remember the best experiments.

COOK! Bread plus leftovers (plus cheese). Pop them into a toaster, or an oven heated to 350° F. The heat will bring out the best flavors. Drizzle herb oil over the finished product.

VARIATIONS. Tomatoes, cheese, and basil oil. Marinated zucchini, Parmesan cheese and onions (sweet or regular) and parsley or thyme oil. Asparagus, bacon, fried egg and parsley or lemon oil. Peach, Brie and basil oil. Apple, arugula, hazelnuts and honey. Arugula, pear and blue cheese. Left over meats can also add great flavors.

shoots

roasted asparagus
raw asparagus salad
blanched kohlrabi marinated in oil
black bean & garlic kohlrabi
pea shoot stir fry
garlic scapes or chutes
braised or "melted" leeks
artichoke stems & savory quinoa salad

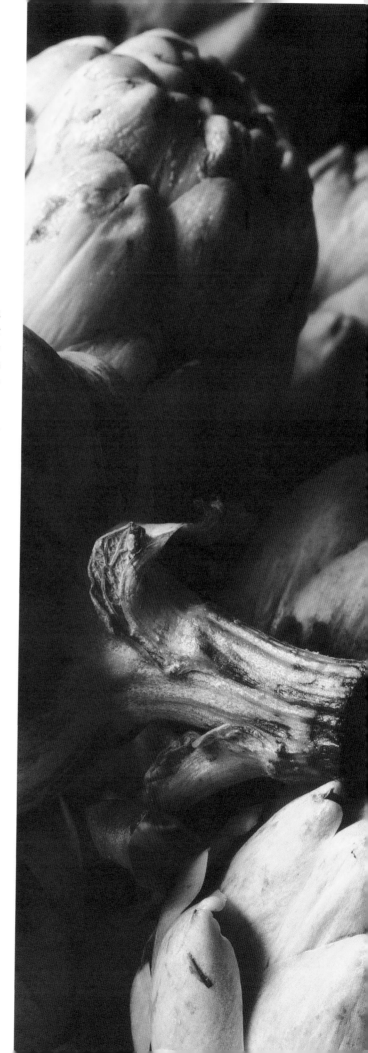

ot many shoots are used in modern cooking, and with good reason. Their main job is to hold up the plant, so they can get tough and woody, especially later in the growing season. But when they first appear, they are tender, short-lived treasures.

Asparagus is the shoot we all know, but your local market may reveal a few surprises.

Things to look for and try: Pea shoots, fennel, garlic chutes or scapes, leeks, artichokes, kohlrabi, and if you are feeling brave, fern fiddle heads (treat them like asparagus). Be brave and discover the next big thing.

PURCHASING.   Look for shoots that appear firm and crisp and a lively green. Stay away from the wilted, spotty and brownish, or anything with mature flowers on the end — those will be tough.

STORAGE.   Keep your shoots in a produce bag or crisper drawer in the refrigerator for no more than a few days. Wash them and trim off any end pieces that look tough or dried out, just before you use them so they don't loose moisture and flavor.

ROASTED ASPARAGUS

SERVES 2 – 4

1 BUNCH ASPARAGUS SPEARS
....
A FEW TSP OF OIL
....

DRESSING:

1 TBS LEMON JUICE
....
2 TBS TASTY OIL
....
1 TSP MUSTARD
....
SALT & PEPPER
....
1 GARLIC CLOVE
....

BAKING PAN
....
STIRRING SPATULA
....
KITCHEN TOWEL
....
SHARP KNIFE (KID KNIFE – OPTIONAL)
....
CUTTING BOARD
....
MEASURING SPOONS
....
SMALL SNAP TOP PLASTIC CONTAINER/
SMALL BOWL
....

Make this when the local asparagus shows up, and revel in that first taste of spring, even when it is still cold outside, maybe with the egg and toast variation to make you warm and cozy inside. Make it a few more times during asparagus season to perfect the technique, or teach the new cooks around you how to do it for you. Easier than pie.

PREP TOGETHER. Rinse the asparagus, and pat dry with the kitchen towel. Break off the thick woody bottoms of your asparagus. Hold the end of the asparagus in one hand and the center in the other. Bend it, the asparagus will break where it starts to get tender. (If you are in a hurry, estimate and chop the whole bunch at once.) Discard the woody ends. Toss the spears with a little oil. Spread them out on the pan.

Make the dressing: Smash, peel and finely chop the garlic clove. In a small container with a tight fitting lid, add all the dressing ingredients. Put on the lid and shake. Check for taste and adjust salt and pepper.

You can also add all the ingredients, except the oil, into a small bowl. Stir them together, and then slowly add the oil while whisking the rest of the ingredients.

COOK!   Heat the oven to 425°F. Place the asparagus in the oven. Cook 15 to 40 minutes depending on the thickness of the asparagus. (They can range anywhere from pencil thin to thick as two fingers!) The asparagus is ready when it looks a little shriveled on the outside, and is floppy when you pick it up. It may even have a few crispy edges. Toss the warm roasted asparagus with the dressing, and serve.

All the thicker spring shoots can be enjoyed this way, and cooked using the "sauté and braise" method (see page 17). Keep your eyes out for fiddleheads, garlic scapes or chutes, ramps, baby leeks, or your own local treasures.

VARIATIONS.   Try the asparagus dressed with just walnut oil, salt, and pepper. Try the asparagus with a fried egg, bacon, and a slice of toast for mopping up. Try roasting some whole, peeled garlic cloves with the asparagus. Serve them with toast to spread them on, or smash them into the dressing.

SUBSTITUTIONS...

No lemon juice?
Vinegar is fine too. I like cider.
Use olive oil, or maybe a nut oil like walnut.

Herbs:
Add 1 – 2 Tbs chopped herbs to the dressing

TRY ASIAN FLAVORING...

1 Tbs rice vinegar
1 Tbs neutral oil
1 Tbs sesame oil
1 tsp soy sauce
1 garlic clove
sesame seeds

RAW ASPARAGUS SALAD

SERVES 3 – 5

1 BUNCH OF ASPARAGUS

1 LARGE HANDFUL VERY WIDE NOODLES
(8 OZ. DRIED)

1 LEMON

TASTY OIL

SALT & PEPPER

SOUP POT

COLANDER

CUTTING BOARD

SHARP KNIFE

VEGETABLE PEELER

KITCHEN TOWEL

SMALL BOWL

SALAD BOWL & SERVING UTENSILS

This is a visually striking dish that causes conversation. Use the freshest asparagus for the sweetest taste. The hot pasta wilts the asparagus, and creates a unique mix of textures. Be ready to explain to everyone what you did.

PREP TOGETHER. Fill the soup pot about $2/3$ full and set over high heat, cover on. Get it boiling. Rinse off the asparagus, and pat dry with the kitchen towel. Break off the thick woody bottoms of the asparagus. Hold the end of the asparagus in one hand, the center in the other, and bend it. The asparagus will break where it starts to get tender. (If you are in a hurry, estimate and chop the whole bunch at once.) Discard the woody ends.

Cut the lemon in half, and squeeze the juice into a small bowl. Cut the bud tops off the spears, slice them in half, and set them aside. Use the vegetable peeler to shave ribbons off the asparagus spears into the large serving bowl. Sprinkle with a pinch of salt, and a drizzle of oil, and toss the ribbons and the sliced tops.

COOK! When the pot is boiling, add the pasta. Stir the noodles a few times to keep them from sticking. Boil them for about 8 minutes. Test a noodle. Not done? Boil a few more minutes. Done? Take the noodles off the heat and pour them into the colander. Right away, add the noodles to the asparagus ribbons, and gently toss to combine.

Add all the lemon juice, and just enough oil (start with 1 or 2 tsp) to keep the noodles from sticking. Add the right amount of salt and pepper for your taste, and serve.

VARIATIONS.   Try substituting brown rice or Israeli or big couscous or other grain for the noodles. Cut the spears in half to make shorter ribbons. Try adding any spare tender leaf herbs that have also shown up for early spring, such as cilantro, basil, parsley, and chives.

SUBSTITUTIONS...

Very thick asparagus spears work best for this recipe.

Oils:
olive
walnut
pistachio

No wide noodles?
Brown rice
Israeli (big) couscous
other grains
But make the ribbons shorter.

Herbs or tender spring greens:
Add those too.

BLANCHED KOHLRABI MARINATED IN OIL

SERVES 4 – 6

1 – 2 KOHLRABI "FLYING SAUCERS"

1 TBS SALT + ¼ TSP SALT

2 GARLIC CLOVES

2 TSP OREGANO

⅛ TSP RED PEPPER FLAKES

3 TBS VINEGAR

½ C TASTY OLIVE OIL

PEPPER TO TASTE

SMALL HANDFUL CHOPPED HERBS

CUTTING BOARD

KNIFE

VEGETABLE PEELER

SOUP POT

LARGE (SLOTTED) SPOON

COLANDER

MEASURING SPOONS

FORK/WHISK

PLASTIC SNAP TOP CONTAINER

This broccoli cousin is very tasty marinated and served cold or at room temperature. It makes a great picnic or "I don't feel like cooking" food. Make at least one day ahead for best flavor, or make lots and have leftovers to pop out of the fridge at a moment's notice for weeks afterwards. Revel in the convenience (and the tastiness) of the leftovers.

PREP TOGETHER.   Clean the kohlrabi. Cut the roots off and the stray sparse leaves. Peel away the tough waxy skin, cutting it in half first may help. Cut into the size pieces you want to eat (large bite size wedges, sticks). Smash, peel and finely chop the garlic cloves.

Mix the dressing: In the covered container, add the vinegar, ¼ tsp salt, chopped garlic, oregano, and red pepper flakes. Whisk in half the oil (or if the lid is tight fitting, put it on and shake). Taste and add any more salt and pepper if they are needed. Mix in the rest of the ½ C oil.)

COOK!   Fill the large pot about half full. Add the 1 Tbs of salt. Bring to a boil. When the water boils, put the prepared vegetables in. Keep them on the heat for about 3 minutes (it doesn't need to return to a boil, the water is plenty hot). Check one piece. When it has softened a little, has lost the "raw" flavor, and can be easily pierced with a knife, but is still crisp — it's perfect. Don't worry, you'll quickly get better at judging this.

Get the vegetables out of the hot water, drain them in the colander, and place them, still hot, in the dressing. Add in the fresh herbs. Cover and refrigerate. These can be used that night or for a few weeks after, and they will just keep getting better.

Note: Blanching, grilling, or otherwise cooking vegetables means breaking down their indigestible (to humans) cell walls allowing us to access many more of their nutrients. The open cell walls also mean they can better absorb the tasty flavors they are soaking in, and the longer the soak, the tastier the bite.

VARIATIONS.   Try this recipe with all sorts of shoots: asparagus, broccoli, celery, or leeks.

Try this with fennel. Cut the bulbs into quarters or eights, cutting out the tough core, and save some of the feather tops. Prepare the bulb the same way as the kohlrabi and use a few handfuls of the feathery fennel fronds as the herb in the marinade.

Try this with root vegetables as well. This blanch and marinate technique works well for carrots, beets, parsnips, turnips, and radishes too. Just make sure you blanch them long enough. Some of the tougher roots take a bit longer. Try green beans or Brussels sprouts. These may only need 2 minutes. Check one early.

Try grilling or roasting zucchini or eggplant (rather than blanching) and place them in the marinade.

The spice mixture is a generic, classic one. Different vegetables and main dishes call out for different spice combinations. Look to the herb oil recipes you've created as one guide.

Try substituting dill, mustard seed, chopped onion, lemon juice, and a little sugar, with chopped thyme. Substitute zucchini and serve them with grilled fish for a Mediterranean spin.

Try a Middle Eastern spin. Keep the garlic, track down a za'atar spice mixture, which is a combination of sumac (a lemony spice), oregano, thyme, salt, and sesame seeds. Use part lemon or lime juice, part mild vinegar for the acid.

Try using the marinated vegetables in the flatbread recipe, or on other sandwiches. Experiment with this recipe, and taste lots to create your own "go to" combination.

▲ These leaves can be cooked and eaten, too!

SUBSTITUTIONS...

Good vinegars for this include:
cider
champagne
red wine
balsamic

Herbs:
basil
oregano
marjoram
chives
thyme
and dried herbs are good too
Italian seasoning is great

BLACK BEAN & GARLIC KOHLRABI

SERVES 2 – 4

1 KOHLRABI "FLYING SAUCER"

2 CLOVES GARLIC

2 TSP OIL

1 TBS BLACK BEAN SAUCE

¼ C WATER

SALT TO TASTE

CHILI SAUCE (OPTIONAL)

CUTTING BOARD

SHARP KNIFE

VEGETABLE PEELER

MEASURING SPOONS

SAUTÉ PAN & LID

STIRRING SPATULA

SUBSTITUTIONS...

Oyster sauce

Chili sauce options:
Sriracha
Tabasco

Black pepper

It looks like a flying saucer, but kohlrabi has the flavor of the sweetest heart of the broccoli stem. Make this to add some Asian flair to your food. Add a pile of sliced, sautéed mushrooms, and/ or add in some quick stir fried beef and serve it with steamed rice to create a complete meal.

PREP TOGETHER.   Pull off any leaves. Cut off fuzzy roots and the pointy top. Cut the kohlrabi in half. Use the vegetable peeler to remove the tough, slightly waxy, outer skin. Cut into bite size pieces. An easy way to do this is cut each half into finger-width slices, then cut the slices into halves or quarters. Smash, peel, and chop the garlic cloves. Stir together the water and black bean sauce.

COOK!   Heat a sauté pan over medium-high heat with the 2 tsp of oil. When you can feel the heat by passing your hand over the pan (about 3 to 4 minutes) or when a piece of kohlrabi begins sizzling, it is ready. Add the garlic, stir a few times, then add the kohlrabi pieces. Stir the kohlrabi over the heat until they start to get tender, about 6 to 8 minutes. Turn down the heat and add the thinned black bean sauce. Stir it into the kohlrabi. Taste. Add salt and pepper, if needed.

VARIATIONS.   Try using oyster sauce instead of black bean sauce, or combine the two for an even richer flavor. Try adding some chopped ginger with the garlic, and sprinkle sesame seeds on at the end.

Try kohlrabi with cheddar cheese. Cut the kohlrabi into bite size pieces or coins. Leave out the black bean sauce, but braise as the recipe directs. When the kohlrabi is fork tender, stir it into small pasta, rice, or other cooked grain. Stir in a large handful or two of grated cheddar cheese for the classic flavor combination.

See the Green Rice recipe on page 18 for rice and grain cooking instructions.

PEA SHOOT STIR FRY

Early in the spring, when you are impatient for peas, track down some tiny shoots and make this green-sweet treat. They taste like the tenderest, tiniest snow pea pods. The shoots you want have 2 to 6 leaves, thin stems, and maybe some tiny curly tendrils. Great with rice and grilled or stir-fried food. Or add mint and create an epic accompaniment for spring lamb.

PREP TOGETHER. Rinse the pea shoots in plenty of water, pat or spin them dry. Peel, smash, and finely chop the garlic clove.

COOK! Heat the sauté pan over medium-high heat with the oil. When you pass your hand over the pan and it feels hot, add the garlic, stir rapidly. After the garlic has sizzled for 15 seconds, add the pea shoots. Stir them until they are a little wilted and tender. Serve immediately.

Until recently pea shoots were only common in Hmong cuisine (an ethnic group from the highlands of Laos and Cambodia). Over the past few years this spring treat has rapidly claimed fans around the globe.

VARIATIONS. Try adding more Asian flavor. Make with 1 tsp of sesame oil, add minced ginger, and use a little chili sauce or sriracha sauce instead of pepper. Sprinkle the finished product with sesame seeds. Try mixing thinly sliced chard or other semi-hearty greens with the pea shoots

Try minty pea shoots: Replace 1 tsp of the oil with butter, use salt, and add a handful of roughly chopped mint leaves halfway through. Leave out the garlic if you want.

Try very early pea shoots that are mostly curly tendrils and tender leaves raw in salads.

SERVES 2 – 4

2 – 3 LARGE HANDFULS PEA SHOOTS

2 TSP OF OIL

1 – 2 CLOVES OF GARLIC

SOY SAUCE OR SALT TO TASTE

SPRINKLE OF PEPPER

CUTTING BOARD

SHARP KNIFE (KID KNIFE – OPTIONAL)

SAUTÉ PAN

STIRRING SPOON

MEASURING SPOONS

KITCHEN TOWELS/SALAD SPINNER

GARLIC SCAPES OR CHUTES

SERVES 4 – 6

1 BUNCH GARLIC SCAPES
2 TSP OIL
SPRINKLE OF SALT & PEPPER
¼ C WATER

CUTTING BOARD
SHARP KNIFE
MEASURING SPOONS
SAUTÉ PAN & LID
KITCHEN TOWELS/SALAD SPINNER

The shoots of the garlic plant appear for a short time in the spring. Enjoy them anywhere you would garlic, and other places regular garlic could never go. Only choose scapes with tightly closed flowers (the stems get tough as the flowers mature). The flavor of the raw scape is sharp like garlic, but the cooked flavor is mellow and slightly sweet.

PREP TOGETHER. Rinse and dry the garlic scapes. Cut the flower buds off the tops of the scapes, and chop them up into 4 or so pieces. They are just as edible as the stem. Slice the stems of the scapes to make thin disks, or on the slight diagonal to make thin ovals. Stop slicing when the stem starts to get tough and woody.

COOK! Heat the sauté pan over medium-high heat with the oil. When you can feel the heat by passing your hand over the pan (or a piece of scape in the oil sizzles happily), add the scapes and a pinch of salt. Stir over the heat for a few minutes until the scapes start to change color. Check for tenderness. If they are tasty, mild, and tender, turn off the heat.

If they are still a bit sharp or tough, add an additional tsp of oil, and cook until they are mild, tender, and tasty. Brown edges are a part of their appeal. Use some immediately on cheese and crackers, or on a sandwich. Store the rest in snap top container in the fridge. Use them everywhere. They should keep for a week or so – instantly ready to go.

VARIATIONS. Try scapes in salads or on cooked greens, on omelets, on soup, on baked or roasted potatoes, in pasta or rice, or as a garnish on fish, chicken or other meats.

Try roasting garlic scapes whole, the same way you would with Roasted Asparagus (see page 36).

Garlic scapes with solid stalks and onion scapes with hollow stalks served with creamy cheeses on crackers. ▶

Preparing onion scapes and topping a pasta dish. ▼

BRAISED OR "MELTED" LEEKS

SERVES 4 – 6

LEEKS (4 BIG OR 6 SMALL)

2 TBS OIL

1 C BROTH

SALT AND PEPPER

WATER

CUTTING BOARD

KNIFE

SAUTÉ PAN & LID

MEASURING CUP

MEASURING SPOONS

Make this the first time you get your hands on some leeks and have about an hour to play in the kitchen. This is one of those recipes that produces a completely unexpected result. Crunchy, slightly oniony shoots transform into a silky, rich, subtly sweet side dish that also works as a sauce. It takes some time, but keeps well, and doesn't require much fussing.

PREP TOGETHER.   Cut the dark green tops off the leeks and discard. From 1 inch or so above the root end, cut the leek shoot into two halves connected at the base. Rinse the layers under running water to make sure there is no grit caught between them. Pat the layers back into place. Cut the root ends off so there are two separate halves.

COOK!   Heat the sauté pan over medium-high heat with the oil for about 4 minutes or until a scrap of leek starts to sizzle. Place the leeks, cut side down, in the oil and cook until they start to brown (about 4 minutes). Carefully turn the leek halves over, and cook again until they start to brown (about another 3 minutes).

Turn the heat down to medium or medium-low. Add the broth, then add water until the liquid is half way up the leeks. Cover with the lid and let it simmer for about 20 minutes. If the leeks are easily pierced with a knife, and have slumped, they have successfully braised or melted. Remove the leeks from the cooking liquid, and set on their serving dish.

Turn the temperature up to boil, and reduce the liquid to about half the amount. Taste the reduced liquid, and add any necessary salt and pepper. Pour over the leeks for serving.

VARIATIONS.   Try the same thing with a big batch of leeks. Brown them on the stovetop the same way, but pop them in a baking dish or pan that they fit into tightly. Increase the liquid to reach 2/3 of the way up the leeks. Dot with a few small pieces of butter or drizzle with a little oil. Bake uncovered in a 325°F oven for 20 to 40 minutes (depends on the leeks), until the tops are golden (or they looked slumped and taste tender and sweet). Use part of them right away, and freeze the rest in small batches for later. Thaw them in the fridge or on the stove or in the microwave. They are so cooked at this point nothing you do is going to "ruin" them.

Try working with smaller pieces. Instead of working with entire half leeks, cut the leeks into smaller pieces (½-inch coins, or cut into 2-inch pieces, then slice into strips). Then melt the leeks in butter or oil instead of broth.

Use twice the oil or butter, but heat the skillet only over medium heat. Add about ½ tsp salt and stir in the smaller pieces of leek. Once the leeks start to wilt, add in ½ a cup of broth, and cover with the lid. Check on them and stir occasionally. If they start to brown on the bottom, turn down the heat. Let it simmer for 20 to 25 minutes or until the leeks are tender and wilted, and taste entirely sweet and luscious. The small pieces freeze and thaw well too.

ARTICHOKE STEMS
& SAVORY QUINOA SALAD

SERVES 4 AS A SIDE DISH

3 SLICES BACON

½ ONION

2-3 ARTICHOKE STEMS

1 C QUINOA

2 C WATER

2 TSP OIL

1 TSP SALT

SALT & PEPPER TO TASTE

CREAM CHEESE

CUTTING BOARD

SHARP KNIFE

SAUCE PAN AND LID

LONG SPOON

PAPER TOWELS

MEASURING SPOONS

VEGETABLE PEELER

The slightly bitter and very green flavor of artichokes works well with a variety of savory flavors. This can be served hot or cold, and works as a side dish, or can be expanded to a main dish. Once you learn the quinoa salad, it can be anything you want.

PREP TOGETHER. Cut the onion in half, peel off the outside layers, cut the onion vertically 3 times from near the root end towards the top, then slice thinly. Chop the bacon into pinky-width sticks or the ham into little cubes.

Peel the tough skin off the stems of the artichokes, cut them in half the long way, then slice into half moons thinner than pinky width.

COOK! Add the 2 tsp of oil to the sauce pan, and place over medium-high heat. Add the bacon or ham. Sauté until the bacon or ham is crisp. Scoop the crispy bits out of the now extra-tasty oil, and set aside on a paper towel. Add the onions and the 1 tsp salt. Sauté until they are brown and soft.

Add the sliced artichokes and quinoa. Stir for a minute or two over the heat to toast the quinoa. Add the liquid, and cover with the lid.

Turn up the heat to bring it to a boil. Turn the heat down to a simmer, and let the quinoa and vegetables cook about 15 minutes. The quinoa is done when it is no longer crunchy, and the seed germs have popped out like little tails.

While the quinoa is still hot, stir in 1 or 2 spoonfuls of your cheese, or stir in a similar amount of tasty oil to make the quinoa creamy. Taste and add salt and pepper to make it delicious. Serve with the bacon sprinkles.

Quinoa (pronounced "keen-wah") is a handy seed to have in the cupboard. As a member of the beet family rather than the grass family, it has a higher protein content than traditional grains. Its quick cooking time and slightly toasty flavor make it a great base for meals — and a wonderful way to transform leftovers.

VARIATIONS. Try letting the quinoa cool (or make the day before). Serve with an herby dressing in place of the cheese or oil.

Dressing for cold salad: 2 Tbs tasty olive oil, 1 Tbs vinegar, 1 tsp mustard, 2 to 4 cloves garlic, a small handful of tender herbs, like parsley, basil, or chives, pinches of salt and pepper.

Try replacing the bacon with mushrooms (shitake are nice, but what you can find will work). Rinse and trim the bottoms of the mushrooms. Pop the stems out and chop them up as small as you can (they are tougher). Roughly chop the caps. Sauté the mushrooms with the onions and leave them in when you cook the quinoa. Follow the rest of the recipe as before.

Try artichoke stems with pasta instead. Add the thinly sliced artichoke stems to the boiling water you are going to cook the pasta in for 10 minutes, then add the pasta. Drain them together. This pasta goes great with the same toppings as the quinoa. Maybe add some tomatoes, fresh or sundried.

Try making other cold salads with quinoa as the base. Arugula, tomato, and cucumber is a good place to start. This is a great way to combine a little of this and a little of that into a satisfying meal.

Try this with baby artichokes. Pull off the tough outer leaves, and cut the artichokes in half. Cut off the leaf tops down to about ½-inch above the "choke" in the middle. Scoop out any fuzzy and spiny bits from the center "choke" with a spoon. Slice the cleaned artichokes the long way, as thin as you can, and proceed with the recipe.

SUBSTITUTIONS...

Meaty flavors:
ham
mushrooms

Cheeses:
goat cheese
tasty oil

Grains:
brown rice
barley
bulgar wheat

flowers

nasturtium & sweet onion flatbread

basil flower fizz

squash blossom pancakes

artichoke petals &
garlic lemon dipping sauce

arugula flower garlic bread

chive flower omelet

ating flowers may seem decadent, exotic, or downright strange. No matter how you view it, it is not something Americans do very often. But they should. Flowers are a delicious treat available to the gardener (all you need is a single pot of chives) and occasionally at the farmers market.

I've included flowers because they are easy to use, fun and tasty to eat, and are a special reward for your own personal efforts in the dirt. I also need to explain that I mainly grow arugula to eat the flowers. The quickest and most vibrant use of flowers is in salads. If the leaves are edible, so are the flowers.

This is a great solution for what to do if you are growing herbs, lettuces or other greens and they bolt (grow tall sprouts and bloom). Not all will be tasty, but they are fine to eat, and some will surprise you (did I mention arugula?). The Green Goddess Salad (see page 10) and A Big Green Salad (see page 8) will both benefit from the addition of arugula flowers, nasturtiums, dandelion blooms, broccoli flowers, or bok-choy flowers. And don't forget the herb flowers, thyme, chives, basil, mint, dill, and cilantro all produce tasty blooms.

STORAGE TIP. Flowers do not store well. It's a pick-and-use proposition. Enjoy them when they appear. If you really need to keep them around, the best bet is to place a piece of barely damp paper towel in a plastic produce bag, drop in the freshly picked blossoms, twist the top closed with plenty of air inside (like a balloon) and refrigerate them, the same way a florist does. They keep for a bit, but don't push it.

NASTURTIUM & SWEET ONION FLATBREAD

MAKE 1 – 2 FLATBREADS PER PERSON

FLATBREAD

1 SWEET ONION

HANDFUL OF NASTURTIUM FLOWERS

TASTY OIL

SALT & PEPPER

SOUP POT

COLANDER

CUTTING BOARD

SHARP KNIFE

VEGETABLE PEELER

KITCHEN TOWEL

SMALL BOWL

SALAD BOWL & SERVING UTENSILS

SUBSTITUTIONS

No time to make flatbread? Try these:
tortillas
pita
chipatis
crepes
lefse

A perfect place for herb oils.

Take the homey base of your flatbread, and turn it into a spectacular display. Thin baguette slices with these toppings make a stunning snack. And once you have tried one flower, how about trying dill flowers and smoked salmon? Cilantro flowers and carnitas shreds? Thyme flowers and sautéed mushrooms?

PREP TOGETHER. Cut the sweet onion in half, peel off the outside layers, and slice thinly. Gently rinse and pat dry the nasturtium flowers. Leave the flowers whole, or roughly chop them.

COOK! Place this all on fresh flatbread, or place on cooled flatbread and toast. Drizzle with a little oil. Sprinkle on the amount of salt and pepper needed to make it just right.

VARIATIONS. Try slicing up some spicy nasturtium leaves and add them as well. Try adding tomatoes, and maybe a few herbs and other flowers (chive or arugula). Try slicing up some squash blossoms instead.

Try adding regular or pickled onions to the squash blossoms and top with cheddar or cotija or feta cheese. For a real Central American spin, sprinkle on some green pumpkin seeds (pepitas) as well.

Note: To quick-pickle onions, use the third variation from The Radish Problem (see page 144). Use cider vinegar for extra punch.

BASIL FLOWER FIZZ

These summer drinks are the prettiest reason to go to the trouble of growing herbs. They can of course be made even when you don't have flowers, but these attractive beverages make any warm day special. It turns out all herb flowers are edible, so be sure to mix and match.

PREP TOGETHER. Pick the basil flowers from the top of the plant and set aside. Pull the leaves off the central stem. Rinse them and pat dry. Tear or roughly chop the leaves. Measure the sugar.

COOK! Add the sugar and water to the sauce pan. Place it over high heat, and stir to dissolve the sugar while bringing it to a boil. As soon as the water boils, turn off the heat and stir in the basil leaves. Set aside to cool. When the syrup is room temperature, strain into a 2 C covered container. Keep on the counter or in the fridge.

Add ice to a tall glass. Add 2 to 4 Tbs syrup to the ice. Add fizzy water while stirring. Drop in a sprig of basil flowers, pushing it into the ice.

VARIATIONS. Try herb lemonade. Add a Tbs of lemon juice for each Tbs of syrup when making the drink. Don't forget the flowers. Rosemary, mint, and lavender all make exceptional lemonades. Try making a lime juice and mint syrup fizz.

Try adding a few sprigs of mint or lemon balm to sun tea and sweetening with a bit of matching herb syrup. Add a few flowers for an extra special summer drink.

SYRUP FOR 6 DRINKS

1 C SUGAR

1 C WATER

1 C BASIL LEAVES

FLOWERS FROM THE BASIL PLANT

ICE

FIZZY WATER

SAUCE PAN

2 C CONTAINER

SIEVE OR COLANDER

STIRRING SPOON

MEASURING CUP

TALL GLASSES

SUBSTITUTIONS...

mint leaves & flowers
lemon balm & flowers
3 Tbs lavender buds
lemon thyme & flowers
rosemary & flowers

SQUASH BLOSSOM PANCAKES 🍴

MAKE 2 – 3 PANCAKES PER PERSON

SQUASH BLOSSOMS
....
1 EGG
....
2 TBS MILK
....
½ TSP SALT
....
1½ TSP SUGAR
....
4 TBS FLOUR
....
BUTTER OR OIL
....
POWDERED SUGAR OR SYRUP
(OPTIONAL)
....

SMALL BOWL
....
FORK/WHISK
....
MEASURING SPOONS
....
MEASURING CUPS
....
SAUTÉ PAN
....
FLAT SPATULA
....
KITCHEN TOWEL
....

When it is time to stop the squash invasion in your garden, make these special pancakes. The blossoms of any zucchini or squash will do — whether it is summer or winter (hard) squash. Don't feel restricted to wheat flour. Use the correct flour for you. Good for breakfast, great for dessert, and a show stopper for brunch when made without sugar for a savory version topped with salsa.

PREP TOGETHER. Pick some squash flowers (2 or 3 per person for breakfast). Remove the large pistil or stamen from the middle (the big thing in the middle of the flower). Rinse and gently pat dry the flowers. Break the egg into the small bowl. Use the fork or whisk to stir together the white and the yolk. Stir in the milk, salt, and sugar. A Tbs at a time, add the flour. This method prevents big lumps (small ones are fine).

Fun fact: Squash plants have male and female flowers. Only the female ones turn into squash, the male ones only provide pollen. Male flowers have a stamen in the center covered with powdery pollen. Female flowers are on a thicker stem (a pre-squash) and the pistil in the middle looks sticky, a little like a brain. That makes it

good for catching pollen — which is its whole job. The pistil and stamen are edible and can be left in, but the texture is very different from the rest of the flower.

COOK!   Place the sauté pan over medium-high heat. Put enough butter or oil in the sauté pan to lightly cover the bottom. After a minute or two, put a drop of batter in the pan. When it starts to sizzle enthusiastically, the pan is ready. Grasp a flower by the stem end, pick up the bowl of batter, and bring them close to the hot pan.

Dip the flower so the outside is well covered, and drape it into the sauté pan. Repeat until the pan is well filled but not crowded. After a minute or two, when the edges of the batter have begun to brown, flip the blossoms over. When the bottom side is brown, and the batter has puffed a bit, remove them to a plate. Enjoy hot, with an optional sprinkle of powdered sugar or drizzle of syrup.

VARIATIONS.   Try this using thin slices of zucchini or summer squash in place of the blossoms. Try leaving out the sugar. Then add chopped onions (sweet or regular) to make this a savory dish. Top with cheese, or serve with tomatoes. Try sliced squash blossoms in a quesadilla or cheese omelet.

SUBSTITUTIONS...

Not eating wheat? Your favorite flour will work just fine here.

rice

corn

chick pea

almond

ARTICHOKE PETALS &
GARLIC LEMON DIPPING SAUCE ℘

ARTICHOKES – 1 PER PERSON

WATER

ARTICHOKES

DRESSING:

¼ C MAYONNAISE OR SOUR CREAM OR
PLAIN YOGURT

2 TBS LEMON JUICE

3 – 6 GARLIC CLOVES

SALT & PEPPER TO TASTE

SMALL HANDFUL OF HERBS

KITCHEN SCISSORS

LEMON CUT IN HALF (OPTIONAL)

STEAMER BASKET (OPTIONAL)

This is the tried-and-true method for enjoying those big prickly globes. Artichokes have enough flavor to be enjoyed plain, but add big flavors to make the most of the unique combination of green, bitter, and mysteriously sweet that is the artichoke. There are tons of mildly nonsensical and time-consuming traditions around preparing artichokes. This recipe pares it down to the basics.

PREP TOGETHER. Fill the medium bowl half way with water, squeeze the lemon into it, and drop in the halves. (Alternatively, pour in a few Tbs of vinegar). Trim an artichoke. Pull off the broken and sad looking leaves around the base until you reach the ones with the pale, spongy flesh at their base. Cut the stems so they make a short handle. (If the stems are long, save them! Toss them into that bowl of lemony water.)

Use a sharp knife, or kitchen scissors to cut off the top of the artichoke fairly flat — so it can stand on its head. The rest of the leaf tops can be trimmed if they have big prickles. Rinse your artichoke, getting your fingers in between the looser outer leaves and give it a good shake to dislodge any dirt.

Drop it in the lemon-water to stop it from browning, and take on the next one. (Stopping the browning is purely cosmetic and doesn't affect the flavor. If you don't do this step, it won't mess up the dish.)

COOK! Fill a large pot to about two inches full with water (about up to the top of your thumb). If you have a steamer basket or rack, pop it in. Bring the water to a boil. Place the artichokes in (or above) the water head down, stem up. Keep the water at a low, steamy boil for 30 to 50 minutes. The time depends on the size of the artichokes, and whether they are tightly packed. The artichokes are done when the base and stems are fork-tender.

While the artichokes are cooking, make the dressing in the small bowl. Smash, peel, and finely chop the garlic. Finely chop any optional herbs. Stir them into the mayo or sour cream (or yogurt). Add salt and pepper and the lemon juice a bit at a time until it is tangy and garlicky and delicious.

Ummmm . . . how do you eat a thistle? When the artichokes are done, remove them with tongs, or a fork through the bottom. Let them drain, and then place them in a bowl, upright. Pull off a leaf, dip the end that was connected to the artichoke into the dressing. Then use your front teeth to scrape the soft flesh off the leaf. The leaves near the center are so tender you can bite off the tasty bit at the bottom.

When you get to the center, there will be tiny spiky leaves, and then fuzz. Use a spoon to scrape out this inedible part, "the choke." The part under the choke is the heart, and contains the greatest concentration of the coveted, mysterious flavor of the artichoke.

Did your artichoke arrive with a long stem? Don't throw that away! The stem is an extension of the tasty heart, and without all the work. A similar flavor can be found in the cardoon, which many assume is the plant the artichoke was developed from.

VARIATIONS. Try adding half of a finely chopped and smashed oil-packed anchovy fillet, or a squirt of anchovy paste to the dressing to make it mysteriously salty and meaty. It's a glimpse into the heart of deeply flavored Mediterranean foods.

Try roasting cleaned baby artichokes like you would asparagus (see page 36). To clean a baby artichoke: Snap off the outside leaves until you reach the ones that are unbroken and have fleshy bases. Cut the dried brown end off the stem. Use a vegetable peeler to remove the tough skin from the stem. With a sharp knife, cut the artichoke into quarters. Use a spoon to scoop out the fuzzy, prickly "choke", and remove the tiniest spiniest leaves.

SUBSTITUTIONS...

No lemon juice?
white wine, cider or rice vinegar works too.

Artichoke friendly herb:
thyme
oregano
mint
or a mix

▲ Grilled baby artichokes with lemons, oil, salt, pepper & red pepper flakes.

▼ Cardoons at the market.

Toss them with a little oil and salt. Roast them for about 15 minutes or until the stem is fork tender. A little char adds unexpected new flavors. Use this dressing or sprinkle with a little bit of lemon juice and eat from the stem up.

Try a sausage stuffed artichoke. Cut the stem off so the artichoke sits flat. Stuff a small meatball-size portion of raw Italian or lamb-mint sausage in each of the big hard leaves, (optionally also poke in a piece of Parmesan or goat cheese). Place the stuffed artichokes head up in the pot, and boil or steam the same way. They'll take about 20 minutes longer.

Try serving the artichoke (stuffed or not) with Green Rice (see page 18) using onion, mint or oregano, and pine nuts. Sprinkle everything with olive oil, salt, and lemon juice.

If you spy cardoons in a market they will look like spiny, dusty-green celery. To clean cardoons: Chop any large leaves off the top, down to where the stalks thicken. Take one of the celery-like stalks from the bunch. Trim outside edges off — the prickles, proto-leaves, and darker green stems. Use a vegetable peeler or paring knife to remove the long silvery strings from the rounded back of the stalk. Cut into finger length pieces. If there is a tough layer on the inside surface, peel it off when cutting the stalks into smaller lengths.

If you are not immediately tossing these into boiling water or steaming them, let them rest in water that has had a lemon squeezed into it, or 3 Tbs vinegar added. Cardoons are also done when fork-tender and no longer crunchy.

ARUGULA FLOWER GARLIC BREAD ❧

Make this if the arugula in the backyard bolts during a super sunny week. Compound butter is one of those things where a fancy name covers up something you already know how to do. Smashing garlic into butter for garlic bread is the compound butter we all make all the time. Here the arugula flowers add a nutty, spicy bite.

PREP TOGETHER.   Take the butter out of the fridge and let it warm up to room temperature. Give the flowers a quick rinse and pat dry. Roughly chop the flowers. Peel and smash the garlic cloves, then chop them very small.

Add the butter in the bowl, and stir it with the fork. Add the garlic and chopped flowers, using the fork to mash them through the butter. Taste, and add a little salt if it needs it.

COOK!   Preheat the oven to 300°F. Slice the bread into your favorite size slices. Spread the compound butter (garlic-arugula flower) one each slice, reassemble the loaf and wrap it in the foil. Heat the bread in the oven for about 15 minutes or until the bread is warm and the butter melting.

VARIATIONS.   Try mixing any other herb flowers, or a mix of flowers. Try a sweet compound butter. Make it with roses (petals only) or pansies (blooms and bases). Add ½ C flowers and ½ C powdered sugar to a food processor, and run until it makes a paste (a couple of minutes). Then add about 1 Tbs of the flower paste to each ¼ C of butter. Try on pancakes or muffins.

MAKES BUTTER FOR 1 LOAF

¼ C BUTTER

2 TBS ARUGULA FLOWERS

3 – 6 CLOVES OF GARLIC

PINCH OF SALT

EXCELLENT BREAD

CUTTING BOARD

KNIFE

BREAD KNIFE (OPTIONAL)

FORK

SMALL BOWL

ALUMINUM FOIL

SUBSTITUTIONS...

Flowers: dill flowers, cilantro flowers
basil flowers, thyme flowers, chive flowers

CHIVE FLOWER OMELET 🌿

MAKE 1 OMELET PER PERSON

1 – 2 EGGS

CHIVES

CHIVE FLOWERS

THIN SLICE OF BUTTER

SALT & PEPPER

KNIFE

CUTTING BOARD

SMALL BOWL

FORK

SAUTÉ PAN

FLIPPING SPATULA

SUBSTITUTIONS...

basil & basil flowers
oregano & oregano flowers
thyme & thyme flowers

This is the perfect meal on a sunny day when the chives are blooming and you want to savor their flavor. Or when you are in a hurry and need a quick, sustaining bite to keep going on a hectic day. Omelets are simple, yet elegant, but the flowers make them special.

PREP TOGETHER. Pick the chive flowers, and a small bunch of chives. Pop the flowers off their stems, and discard the stems (they get tough). Chop the chives small, and separate the blooms from the flower ball. Break the egg(s) into the small bowl. Use the fork to break the yolk, then stir briskly until the egg is a fairly uniform light yellow. Stir in a pinch of salt and pepper.

COOK! Put the thin slice of butter in the sauté pan, then place it over medium-high heat. Spread the butter around as it melts. The pan is ready when the butter melts, then bubbles.

Pour the beaten egg into the pan. Tip the pan to cover the bottom. Watch, but don't fuss with it. When the edges are solid, but the center is still a bit runny, sprinkle most of the chives in the center of the omelet.

Fold the omelet like a letter, a third into the center, then the other third. Count to 20, flip the omelet over and count to 20 again. Slide the omelet onto a plate, sprinkle with the rest of the chives and the chive flowers. Enjoy!

VARIATIONS. Try the same thing with other herbs and their flowers, or a mix of herbs and flowers.

fruits

stone fruit cake with
ginger cream cheese frosting

baked ginger pluots

clafouti (fruit flan)

strawberry butter

cottage cheese pancakes

summer berry pie bars

granita – cucumber melon

nectarine & sweet onion relish

fruits love cheese (& nuts)

ginger shortbread & stone fruit

fruit scones

applesauce

smoothies

a few bites of tomato

toasted tomato sandwich

grilled cheese & tomato sandwich

oven roasted summer squash

summer squash, cabbage
& sweet onion salad

seasonal minestrone soup

zucchini pancakes two ways

sesame soy zucchini

Mexican chocolate zucchini bread

baked delicata winter squash

sweet & spicy butternut squash soup

SWEET & SAVORY

cience teacher wins! If it grows on a plant where the flower used to be, it is a fruit. Peaches, apples, cucumbers, pumpkins, and the poor beleaguered tomato are all just seed delivery vessels, doing their part to give the next generation the best possible start. Don't worry, the fruits have been divided into familiar categories:

Sweet. What we normally think of as fruit.

Savory. Produce we treat as vegetables.

Fruits, like leaves, can be roughly divided into sensible groups.

Stone fruits. Single-seed fruits like cherries, peaches, nectarines, apricots, plums and their many hybrids.

Berries. Bite sized, many seeded fruits, anything with the word 'berry' in the name like strawberry, raspberry, blueberry, blackberry, marionberry, and gooseberry.

Summer Squashes. Zucchini and other yellow things that look like zucchini. They come in a variety of shapes and sizes, such as ball, patty pan or flying saucer, or crookneck.

Winter or Hard Squashes. Anything even vaguely resembling a pumpkin. They have a hard skin, orangy flesh and a hollow chamber with seeds attached to strings inside. They come in a bewildering, and entertaining variety. Some are familiar looking, like butternut, delicata, sunshine, spaghetti, Cinderella, and acorn. Then there are several rather alien-looking varieties such as blue banana, ghost, turban, and warty.

Finally, there is the waterfall of tomato, cucumber, apple, and melon varieties that round out this massive and enjoyable group.

Of course most fruits can be enjoyed raw, or barely touched, but sometimes the summer goodness comes in avalanche proportions. After eating all the perfectly ripe nectarines we can, over the sink (slurp!), it is time for a few recipes. If you are looking for ways to preserve produce, check out the Smoothie recipe (see page 84), or for preserving larger amounts, see the Bibliography on page 150.

Are there more categories of fruits? Yes.

Are they covered in this book? No.

Why not? Many are either atypical in most of North America, already extremely familiar, or not usually found at a farmers market, and I had to stop somewhere and finish the book.

Enjoy the freedom to experiment for yourself, ask questions at the market, or check the Bibliography for more thorough volumes.

BERRIES

PURCHASING.   They should be ripe when you buy them. These do not get riper after picking.

STORAGE.   Purchase only what you will use *very soon* or *freeze right away.*

Berries are delicate packages at their peak for only a moment. Then they happily rot into compost for the seeds inside. You can refrigerate them (unwashed) for a day or two. To freeze, gently rinse, pat dry, freeze in single layers on large pans. When solid, store in zip top bags with the air squeezed out.

STONE FRUITS

PURCHASING.   They fall into two categories: Ripe right now and ripe soon.

Ripe right now. It smells like what it is (peach, nectarine, apricot) and the flesh gives under gentle pressure. Or, more exactly, it makes you want to eat it right now. Cherries are the right color when they are ripe.

Ripe soon. It still smells like what it is, but is firm to rock-hard. If a peach does not smell like a peach, it never will. It may get soft, but it will be mealy and it will never taste right.

STORAGE.   If you aren't going to eat it right now or by the next morning, don't buy anything perfectly ripe. Refrigeration will slow down the progress to overripe only a little.

Cherries are a little more stable, and can keep (unwashed and bagged) in the refrigerator for up to a week. You can freeze by slicing or pitting. Peel peaches, halve or slice all larger stone fruits, and pit cherries before freezing. Freeze prepared fruit in a single layer in a large flat pan. When solid, seal in a zip-top bag with the air squeezed out. Perfect for smoothies and cooked applications.

To ripen, under-ripe fruit should be stored in the fridge for up to 5 days in a plastic bag or until you want to ripen it. Then it goes on the counter in a paper bag with other fruits. Check daily. It can go from stony to perfect to squashy in an alarmingly short amount of time.

MELONS

PURCHASING. Melons behave much like stone fruits. The ones you want to buy are either ready now, or ready soon. Never buy one that has no melon smell. Also shy away from ones that already have squishy spots.

The best bets are:

The smell test. Does it smell wonderful? If so, it's ready! Smell slightly of melon? Ready soon. Not like melon at all? It will never be good (the melon was too green when picked).

The heavy test. Does it feel heavier than it should? Great! Too light? Put it back.

STORAGE. Refrigerate anything you aren't going to eat right away, or ripen. Keep an eye on the under ripe ones as they also transition quickly.

You can freeze by peeling and slicing into chunks. Freeze prepared fruit in a single layer in a large flat pan. When solid, seal in a zip top bag with the air squeezed out. Perfect for smoothies and cooked applications.

To ripen, leave the melon out on the counter. When they smell like melon and feel extra heavy the melon is ready. Cut ripe melon can be covered and refrigerated for a few days.

STONE FRUIT CAKE WITH
GINGER CREAM CHEESE FROSTING ⌒∕

ENOUGH FOR 8 – 12 SERVINGS

RIPE STONE FRUIT – AT LEAST 2

¾ C CORNMEAL

1 C FLOUR

½ C SUGAR

2 TSP BAKING POWDER

½ TSP SALT

1 C MILK

1 EGG

2 TBS BUTTER

FROSTING:

½ C CREAM CHEESE

2 – 3 TBS CREAM OR MILK

2 – 4 TBS POWDERED SUGAR

1 – 2 TSP GROUND GINGER

CANDIED OR CRYSTALLIZED GINGER
(OPTIONAL)

LARGE BOWL

2 SMALL BOWLS

MEASURING SPOONS

MEASURING CUPS

CUTTING BOARD

SHARP KNIFE

FORK /WHISK

PIE PLATE (8 OR 9 INCH) OR 2 LOAF PANS

Any stone fruit fits in this cake, plums, pluots, nectarines, peaches, apricots, apriums, and so on. It is a great way to share fruit when there is plenty, or too much right this second. Cooled and wrapped tightly, the cake freezes, giving you a way to share perfectly ripe fruit a little later. Bonus, it is practically cornbread, so it could be breakfast too.

PREP TOGETHER.   In the big bowl, measure out all the dry ingredients (corn meal, flour, sugar, salt, baking powder), and stir together. Melt the butter, and set it aside to cool enough to touch. Crack the egg into the small bowl, whisk to scramble the egg, and stir in the milk. Cut the stone fruit into slices as thin as your pinky, or thinner. (If using peaches, peel them if you don't like fuzzy skin.)

Frosting: Stir the cream cheese to loosen it. (Use regular or low fat cream cheese. Non-fat cream cheese may split or taste odd.) Stir 1 Tbs of cream or milk into the cream cheese. Stir in more cream or milk a little at a time until it has a nice spreadable texture. Add the ground ginger and sugar until the frosting tastes just right. If you have candied or crystallized ginger, slice and dice it small, and stir it into the frosting. Set aside. (Cover and refrigerate if you need to.)

COOK!   Heat the oven to 375°F. Spread a thin layer of butter or oil on the pie plate (cooking spray is fine too). Stir the wet ingredients (milk, egg, butter) into the dry ingredients. Pour the batter into the buttered or oiled pan. Layer the sliced fruit over the top of the cake. Overlap slices if there is lots of fruit. Bake for 30 to 35 minutes. Check the center of the cake with a knife. If the knife has batter on it, the center is not set. Bake another 5 minutes and check again.

When the cake is firm, the edges are browning and the knife comes out clean, set the cake on the counter to cool. Eat it nice and warm with the ginger frosting. Wrap any unfrosted extras, after they have cooled, and place in a zip-top bag. Freeze for later. Warm in a 300°F oven until heated through (or microwave).

BAKED GINGER PLUOTS &

This is a great topping for ice cream, yogurt, waffles, pancakes, French toast or anything else that needs a tart, fruity lift. Nectarines, plums, cherries, and other firm, tart fruits can all stand in for the pluots. Once cooked, these can be frozen until they are needed, again, giving you a calmer way to deal with ripe fruit, other than chasing down family and friends to make them "eat it now, before it goes bad!"

PREP TOGETHER.   For each 3 or 4 pluots, use a piece of ginger about the size of the top joint of your thumb. Peel the ginger, slice it thinly, and cut those pieces into matchstick size strips. Cut the fruit in half, twist the halves to remove the pits, then slice the halves into sixths, eighths, or other bite-size pieces.

COOK!   Heat the oven to 325°F. Combine the fruit, ginger, and sugar in the pan. Bake for about 12 minutes. If the fruit has softened and is releasing juice, it is close to done. If the fruit is still firm, give it a few more minutes. Taste test to be sure.

When the fruit is ready, serve it over something cold, like ice cream, yogurt, sorbet, or granita. Or use it as topping for your favorite breakfast food such as Squash Blossom Pancakes (see page 54) or Cottage Cheese Pancakes (see page 70). Ginger Shortbread Cookies (see page 78) are a great addition. Extras can be refrigerated or frozen for later use.

VARIATIONS.   Try using berries that are a little too tart. Try with apples. Try leftovers in smoothies.

4 PLUOTS MAKE ½ C

RIPE PLUOTS
....

1 TSP SUGAR FOR EACH PLUOT
....

FRESH GINGER
....

CUTTING BOARD
....

SHARP KNIFE
....

PARING KNIFE
....

LARGE BAKING PAN
....

MEASURING SPOONS
....

VEGETABLE PEELER (OPTIONAL)
....

SUBSTITUTIONS...

Fruits:

plums

apriums

apricots

sour cherries

nectarines

peaches

tart berries

or a mix

Leftovers are tasty in smoothies.

CLAFOUTI (FRUIT FLAN)

I don't know if I first had this for dessert or breakfast as a child, but it doesn't matter. It is spectacular as both. And don't worry, all fruits are the right fruits for what is essentially a fancy looking baked pancake.

PREP TOGETHER. Wash the fruit and cut it up, if needed. Measure out and mix together the dry ingredients in the large bowl. Crack the eggs into the small bowl, and beat together with the fork or whisk. Add in the rest of the liquid (milk, vanilla) ingredients.

COOK! Heat the oven to 350°F. Use the butter or oil to lightly grease the bottom of the pan. Stir the wet ingredients into the dry. Use the fork to thoroughly stir all the ingredients together until smooth. (Alternately add all the ingredients, except the fruit, to a blender, and run for about 45 seconds, until the batter is smooth.)

Pour about half the batter into the pie plate, scatter the fruit, then cover with the rest of the batter. Bake for about 40 minutes. It is done when puffed up and browned, and a knife cut into the center comes out clean. Serve hot from the oven or at room temperature or reheated later.

VARIATIONS. Try spiked clafouti. As a classic French dessert, there are plenty of options for adding liqueurs to enhance different fruit flavors. Pair a fruit with 3 Tbs liqueur, and let the fruit soak in the liqueur and ¼ C sugar for an hour before making the clafouti. Strain the sweetened liquid off the fruit, and add milk to that to make up the ¾ C total liquid for the recipe. Subtract ¼ C sugar from the original recipe as well.

The classic French version is made with sour "pie cherries" (often the Montmorency variety in the United States) with the pits still in! If you get a chance to try it this way, do it. Just sprinkle an extra ¼ C of sugar over the surface before baking it in the oven.

STRABERRY BUTTER

I am divulging family secrets here, but having strawberry joy in February is more than worth spilling the beans. Strawberry butter is why my mom would make us pick 10 times the amount of strawberries we could possibly eat before they went bad. My first few years of picking — almost none of the berries made it to the box. I'm a little better now.

PREP TOGETHER. Let the butter sit on the counter until it is room temperature. Rinse the strawberries. Cut off the green tops, and remove the white cores. Pushing a drinking straw through the pointy end of the strawberry up towards the top will capture the core and leaves all in one (and make the task fun for kids).

COOK! Put the strawberries in the large bowl, squash them with the fork to break them up, and release lots of juice. Add the powdered sugar slowly to avoid producing a sugar cloud, or splattering juice, and stir it into the strawberries.

Add the butter. Use the fork or mixer or potato masher to incorporate the butter and sugar strawberry mix. If the strawberries are very juicy, add more butter and sugar (in equal parts) to absorb and incorporate all the juice. You'll know it is about right when the butter is pink and there is a limited amount of leftover strawberry "syrup."

Spoon the strawberry butter into the lidded containers. Keep one in the fridge to enjoy over the next few days. Keep the rest in the freezer and bring them out as needed. There's something special about this fresh strawberry flavor in February.

We always ate this with Cottage Cheese Pancakes (see page 70).

This recipe only works with the super juicy, short season strawberries that don't travel well. You know you have the right strawberries if they stain everything they touch red, and start looking tired the next morning. Make this recipe the day you get these strawberries or the next day.

1 C STRAWBERRIES MAKES
2 C STRAWBERRY BUTTER

A PROPORTIONAL RECIPE:

FOR EACH 1 C LOCAL STRAWBERRIES
....
APPROXIMATELY 1 C POWDERED SUGAR
....
1 C BUTTER
....

MEASURING CUP
....
COLANDER
....
SMALL KNIFE
....
FORK/STAND MIXER/POTATO MASHER
....
LARGE BOWL
....
TIGHTLY LIDDED FREEZABLE
CONTAINERS – SMALLER IS BETTER.
....

COTTAGE CHEESE PANCAKES

ABOUT 24 PANCAKES,
4 – 8 PER PERSON

3 EGGS

¼ C FLOUR

2 TBS OIL

¼ TSP SALT

1 C COTTAGE CHEESE

½ TSP VANILLA

OIL OR BUTTER

BLENDER
OR LARGE BOWL & FORK/WHISK

MEASURING CUPS

MEASURING SPOONS

SAUTÉ PAN

FLIPPING SPATULA

SUBSTITUTIONS...

Not eating wheat?
Lots of flours work well. Try:
rice
corn
coconut
almond

Make these "Silver Dollar" style pancakes no larger than the palm of your hand.

PREP TOGETHER.   Put all the ingredients into the blender. Put on the lid and run the blender until the batter is smooth, about a minute. (No blender? Beat the eggs in a large bowl, stir in the cottage cheese, smashing the curds with the fork, then stir in the oil, salt, and flour).

The flour is here mainly for its starchy properties, wheat flour is not essential. Other starchy flours, like rice, will serve.

COOK!   Heat the sauté pan over medium to medium-high heat (adjust as you go along) with a little oil or butter in the bottom. After about 3 minutes place a drip of batter in the pan. The pan is ready when the batter sizzles nicely.

Pour about 3 Tbs of batter into the sauté pan to make pancakes about the size of the palm of your hand. Let them cook until they get bubbles in the top. Flip and cook about 30 more seconds. They should still be a bit creamy in the middle.

Eat nice and warm, spread with strawberry butter. (Or keep warm in an oven that has been heated to 300°F, then turned off.)

SUMMER BERRY PIE BARS

MAKES 3 DOZEN BARS

CRUST AND TOPPING:

3 C FLOUR

1½ C SUGAR

½ TSP SALT

1½ C BUTTER

FRUIT FILLING:

4 LARGE EGGS

2 C SUGAR

1 C SOUR CREAM

3/4 C ALL PURPOSE FLOUR

PINCH SALT

2 LBS. BERRIES

CUTTING BOARD

SMALL SHARP KNIFE

MEASURING CUPS

MEASURING SPOONS

3 MIXING BOWLS – LARGE, MED.& SMALL

PASTRY BLENDER OR TWO BUTTERKNIVES

FORK OR WHISK

HALF-SHEET PAN OR TWO 9 X 13 PANS

KITCHEN TOWEL

I found my first version of this recipe in Rebecca Rather's, *The Pastry Queen*. It turns out they are perfect for all sorts of berries, and really, all sorts of summer fruits. Mmmmm . . . fruit pies! No fussy crust and a bake sale best seller.

PREP TOGETHER. If you're using frozen fruit, thaw in the fridge overnight, and drain in a colander before using. Heat the oven to 350°F. For the crust, stir together the flour, sugar, and salt. Cut the cold butter into pieces about the size of the top joint of your thumb (½-inch pieces). Add the butter to the flour mixture. Using the 2 knives, pastry blender, or clean hands, cut the butter into smaller and smaller pieces, into the flour mixture, until the whole mixture looks crumbly. (Or pulse the crust ingredients in a food processor, to get the same result.)

Scoop out 2 C of the mixture, place in a small bowl, and put that in the fridge. Pour the rest into the half sheet pan (or divide between the two pans), and press down with clean hands into an even layer. Bake in the oven for 12 to 15 minutes until it is light golden brown. Set aside, cover with a kitchen towel, and let it rest until cool to the touch.

For the fruit filling, rinse and pat dry fresh berries, or make sure frozen berries are thawed and drained.

COOK! Make sure the oven is back at 350°F. In the large bowl, briskly stir the eggs with the fork or whisk. Then stir in the sugar, salt, sour cream and flour. Gently stir in the prepared fruit. Pour the fruit mixture over the top of the cooled crust. Then sprinkle the reserved 2 C of crust mixture from the fridge over the top. Bake for 44 to 55 minutes or until the top is lightly browned.

To cut into bars, this must cool for at least an hour. If you want to enjoy it right away, spoon it out like a cobbler while it is hot (yummy with ice cream!). The bars will also freeze for up to 2 months if tightly wrapped. Thaw these in the fridge and then let them warm up to room temperature or warmed in a toaster oven.

VARIATIONS. Try with any ripe summer fruit — again fresh or frozen works. Just be sure to remove any inedible bits (large seeds, tough or fuzzy skins, stems), and cut the fruit down to berry, or bite-sized pieces.

Peaches or plums. Add 1 to 2 tsp of ground ginger to the "crust" mixture.

Apricots. Stir 3 Tbs of orange marmalade into the fruit filling.

Cherries. Remember to pit them first!

Apples. Add 1 Tbs cinnamon and ½ tsp allspice to the crust.

SUBSTITUTIONS...

Plain yogurt, especially whole milk, stands in very well for sour cream.

You can make this in the winter too. Just use frozen berries.

GRANITA — CUCUMBER MELON

ENOUGH FOR 8 – 12 SERVINGS

2 CUCUMBERS – BANANA SIZE

1 SMALL HONEYDEW TYPE MELON

4 TBS SUGAR (MORE OR LESS)

JUICE OF 1 LEMON (¼ C)

1 TBS VODKA OR OTHER CLEAR LIQUOR

KNIFE

VEGETABLE PEELER

CUTTING BOARD

BLENDER/FOOD PROCESSOR

8 X 8 INCH (OR SIMILAR) METAL PAN OR
FREEZABLE PLASTIC CONTAINER

METAL SPOON

FORK

MEASURING SPOONS

This is the perfect answer to Popsicle cravings when you have a counter full of summer fruit. When you are hot, this is cool. Yes! Make all sorts of other flavors too.

PREP TOGETHER. Peel and cut the ends off the cucumbers. Cut them in half so they look like boats and scoop out the seeds. Chop them into pieces about as thick as your thumb, toss in the blender.

Discard the seeds out of the center of the melons. Scoop the flesh and juice off the rind into the blender. The honeydew-type melon should be super juicy and sweet when you do this. This is a perfect way to use up the end of a melon that is approaching too soft.

Add the lemon juice, and blend. Add the sugar 1 Tbs at a time, blend and taste. Add enough sugar so it tastes a little too sweet. (If the melon was crunchy, you may need extra sugar.) Add the Tbs of vodka and blend one more time.

FREEZE! Pour the liquid into the pan, pop it in the freezer, and check at 45 minutes to an hour to see how fast it is freezing. Stir the frozen parts in with the still liquid parts. Check again in an hour or so. If it is still slushy, stir again, and return awhile later. When it is solid-ish, run a fork over the frozen stuff. If it turns into the ice equivalent of cotton candy, you have granita.

Scrape what you want off with a fork and enjoy. To store for longer, scrape it all into the fluffy state. Spoon it into freezable containers with tight lids. Use like ice cream or sorbet or sherbet. If the granita freezes into something suitable for ice carving, it needs more sugar. Thaw it either gently on the stove or in the microwave, or overnight in the fridge. Then stir in a few more Tbs of sugar and try again.

The cucumbers need to be firm, sweet, and juicy. Stay away from huge arm-sized cucumbers; they can be woody and bitter.

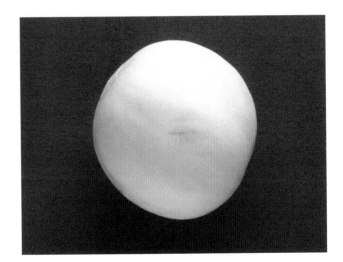

Why the liquor and extra sugar? Both of the sugar and alcohol molecules lower the freezing temperature of water by getting between the water molecules and interfering with the formation of ice crystals. They also help make the "grainy" texture that granita is named for by keeping the crystals that do form fairly small. The room temperature liquid should taste a little too sweet since cold has a deadening effect on taste buds. If you want to leave out the alcohol, its anti-freeze properties can be replaced by adding a bit more sugar.

VARIATIONS. Granita is a blank canvas just waiting for you to make something up. Try using the herb flavored simple syrups (see page 21) as your sugar. And a splash of flavoring extract can create interesting flavor additions.

In all cases you will need 3 to 4 C loosely packed fruit. Be sure to remove all non-edible seeds. Remove any thick or gritty peels (like melon rinds, fuzzy peach and apricot skin, and apple and pear skins) to keep frustrating bits out of the granita that won't melt.

Try a super special summer slushy. On a particularly hot day, fill a glass with granita, and pour in enough lemonade, limeade or other citrus juice to make a fabulous, fruity, spoon-ready slush.

Try a grown-up slushy. Replace part of the juice with limoncello. Try strongly flavored liquors in place of the vodka to create an interesting hint of flavor. Almond liquor with cherries, gin with the cucumber-melon, orange liquor with the peach blackberry, etc.

SUBSTITUTIONS...

Granita is a blank canvas for flavors. Try:

cantaloupe – plum

peach – blackberry

cherry – nectarine

strawberry – basil

pear – shiso (or cinnamon)

Possibly fennel – beet – orange?

make up your own

Try replacing the sugar with an herb syrup for even more flavor. Use 5 Tbs instead of 4.

NECTARINE & SWEET ONION RELISH

MAKES ABOUT 1 C

1 FIRM NECTARINE

1 SMALL SWEET ONION

2 TBS MILD VINEGAR

2 TBS WATER

1 TBS CHOPPED FRESH BASIL

PINCH OF SUGAR (OPTIONAL)

SALT & PEPPER

CUTTING BOARD

SHARP KNIFE (KID KNIFE – OPTIONAL)

MEDIUM SIZED BOWL

MEASURING SPOONS

At some point in the summer, even the most dedicated fruit eater needs a break from sweet alone. This brings fruit to the dinner table in a way that enhances meats and other savory flavors. Oh, and don't stop with nectarines. Peaches, plums, apricots and other fruits can all make their way into a relish. (It turns out to also be a good place to use not quite ripe fruit.)

PREP TOGETHER. Cut the onion in half through the root. Peel off the outer dry layers, and slice the sweet onion thin. Coarsely chop the herbs, and stir into the vinegar or white wine.

Slice the nectarine around the equator then cut into 12 or 16 slices. You want fairly small slices — this is a relish, to be eaten along with something else.

COOK! Combine all the ingredients. If you were thinking ahead, let this sit for a few hours or overnight. This was created for crab, and is good with fish, poultry, salty ham, and sharp cheeses.

VARIATIONS. Other fruit works too. Peaches and firm plums are good choices. Try mixing in some parsley, thyme, and oregano with the basil, or replacing it. Try adding a little heat with a hot pepper, and if you add some chopped tomato, all of a sudden it is salsa.

FRUITS LOVE CHEESE (& NUTS)

Cooking with fruit, and enjoying it plain are both important. But sometimes a quick, tasty, complete snack is all that you really need. Combining sweet, juicy summer fruit with savory cheese and crunchy nuts creates fantastic flavor combinations that also just happen to be quick and incredibly healthy.

PREP TOGETHER.   Slice ripe fruit and pair it with some protein. As a kid, one of the most perfect snacks was apples and peanut butter. At 2:30 P.M. in the afternoon, when I realize lunch has passed me by, it still is. Even better, there's more than peanut butter out there!

VARIATIONS.   Use nut butters to spread on your fruit. Try unsweetened nut butters to let the flavors of the fruit shine through.

Try it with a variety of cheeses. Goat cheese and other soft, fresh cheeses work with anything. They are also great with vegetables. Ricotta, cottage cheese, mascarpone and other soft cheeses are great for spreading on fruit and for baking.

RIPE FRUIT

CHEESE

NUTS OR NUT BUTTER

CUTTING BOARD

KNIFE

SUBSTITUTIONS...

Nut Butters: almond butter, cashew butter or sunflower seed butter

Cheeses:
Cheddar, sharp cheeses, with tart fruits
Brie, soft cheeses with rinds, with sweet fruits
Mozzarella and string cheese with tomatoes
Blue cheese with pears and apples

GINGER SHORTBREAD & STONE FRUIT ❧

MAKES ABOUT 24 SMALL COOKIES

1 C BUTTER

¾ C POWDERED SUGAR

2 C FLOUR

1 TSP SALT

2 TSP GROUND GINGER

2 TBS CANDIED
OR CRYSTALIZED GINGER

PASTRY BLENDER OR 2 BUTTER KNIVES

LARGE BOWL

SMALL BOWL

PLASTIC WRAP OR BAG

BAKING SHEETS

MEASURING CUPS

MEASURING SPOONS

FLIPPING SPATULA

SHARP KNIFE

PAPER TOWEL WITH A LITTLE OIL ON IT

CUTTING BOARD

ROLLING PIN – OR HANDY CYLINDER

STAND MIXER (OPTIONAL)

As party fare, sliced fruit for dessert can seem a little too effortless. But pairing it with ginger shortbread elevates the cookie, and gives your summer fruit something to stand (sit?) on. Shortbread freezes like a dream, so make lots of cookies ahead of time while pondering summer's treasures. When the fruit shows up, thaw the cookies, or toast them lightly when feeling truly decadent.

PREP TOGETHER. Chop the candied ginger into tiny pieces (wiping the knife with an oily paper towel will reduce sticking). Candied ginger is chunks of ginger root that have been soaked in a dense sugar syrup. They are still soft and chewable, and sticky when chopped. It can usually be found at Trader Joe's markets and many Asian groceries. Crystallized ginger is usually sliced and dried. It is much tougher, and typically has a stronger ginger bite. This can be found at nearly any grocery store and in Asian groceries. Both add excellent flavor.

In the small bowl, stir together the dry ingredients (flour, salt, and ground ginger). Cut the butter into small pieces with the knives, then use clean hands to squish together the powered sugar and the butter until butter has absorbed all the sugar (or cream together the sugar and butter in the mixer).

Add the flour mixture to the sugary butter, and use the two knives to cut the butter into smaller and smaller pieces, until it sticks together as a dough. (Or, slowly add the flour in the mixer. Stop as soon as it just combined so the cookies aren't tough.)

Form the dough into a flattened ball, wrap it in plastic, and place it in the refrigerator for at least 30 minutes. You can do this part several days ahead. But set the dough on the counter for 30 minutes so it is no longer in the "rock-hard" state for baking.

COOK! Heat the oven to 325°F. Grease the baking sheets with butter or oil or cooking spray. Clear off some counter space and get it a little floury. Roll out the dough to about ¼-inch thick. Either slice the cookies into simple shapes (squares, triangles, diamonds) with a butter knife, or use cookie cutters.

Use a spatula to transfer the cookies onto the greased baking sheet, and place in the oven. Bake for 14 to 18 minutes or until just light brown around the edges.

VARIATIONS. Try freezing some of the dough for much later. After it has been in the fridge for the 30 minutes, divide it in half and roll the dough into two logs with a diameter about the length of your thumb. Wrap it in plastic wrap or wax, parchment or freezer paper. Place these in a zip top bag and freeze. When you want to make cookies, let the log sit out for about 5 minutes at room temperature, and use a thin bladed knife to slice off pieces about the width of

your pinky. Bake a little longer; they are done when browned on the bottom but still very light on top.

Try leaving out the ginger for plain shortbread. Try other flavors of shortbread. Savory ones give a twist to appetizers.

Try cheddar bacon shortbread. (Reduce the sugar to ½ C , add ½ C (1.5 oz.) grated cheddar cheese and add $^1/_3$ C finely chopped bacon) and serve with tomatoes that have been sliced and sprinkled with salt and pepper.

Try Havarti dill shortbread. Reduce the sugar to ½ C, add ½ C (1.5 oz.) grated Havarti cheese, and add 2 Tbs finely chopped fresh dill. Serve with smoked salmon.

Try kale, Parmesan and dried tomato shortbread. Reduce the sugar ½ C, add ½ C (1.5 oz.) grated Parmesan, 2 Tbs finely chopped kale and 2 Tbs finely chopped dried tomatoes. Serve with pesto and/or roasted root vegetables.

Try citrus shortbread. Add the zest from small citrus fruits or half of large ones, such as lemon, lime, tangerine, 4 kumquats, Buddha hand, orange, and grapefruit.

Try rosemary garlic shortbread. Reduce sugar to ½ C, add 2 Tbs rosemary and 1 to 2 cloves garlic, both finely chopped. Serve with strongly flavored cured meats such as salami, thinly sliced hams, or prosciutto.

Experiment!

FRUIT SCONES

MAKES 6 – 8 SCONES

1 C FLOUR

1 TSP BAKING POWDER

¼ TSP SALT

1 TBS SUGAR PLUS 1 TSP

4 TBS BUTTER

1 EGG

3 TBS CREAM OR MILK

½ C OR SO BERRIES OR SLICED FRUIT

MEDIUM BOWL

MIXING BOWL

MEASURING CUPS

MEASURING SPOONS

FORK

TWO BUTTER KNIVES (OPTIONAL)

MIXING SPOON OR
RUBBER SPATULA

BAKING SHEET

CUTTING BOARD

SHARP KNIFE

This classic teatime snack is excellent any time of day. Yesterday's scones make one of the best summer breakfasts. Berries, plums, peaches, pluots, or pears all make delicious treats. Scones are even good plain but are even better with what's sweet now. (Psst, they are also great with frozen fruit.)

PREP TOGETHER. Add the dry ingredients (flour, baking powder, salt and sugar) to the larger bowl. Stir together to mix. Cut the butter into ½-inch pieces. Add it to the dry ingredients.

With clean hands or two butter knives, cut the butter into smaller and smaller pieces on the flour mixture. Continue breaking up the butter until it is tiny and well coated with flour. The flour mixture should now look like it has large grains in it. In the small bowl, use the fork to beat the egg, then stir in the cream. Rinse the fruit, slice larger fruit into bite-sized pieces.

COOK! Preheat the oven to 425°F. Add the liquids to the dry ingredients, and stir about 10 times with the spoon. Do NOT make the batter smooth. Lumps are okay.

Place the fruit on top of the batter. Gently fold the batter over the fruit a few times. Gentle! Pour and scrape the soft, sticky dough out onto the baking pan. With floury hands, pat the dough into a circular shape about ¾-inch thick. With one of the butter knives divide the circle into 6 or 8 pieces. Leave them where they were cut. Sprinkle the extra 1 tsp of sugar over the top. Large crystal sugar (for example, Sugar in the Raw, turbinado, etc.) is fun and crunchy here.

Place the pan in the oven for 16 to 22 minutes. The scones will be slightly puffed, firm, and lightly browned. A toothpick should come out of the scones clean when they are done.

VARIATIONS. This recipe doubles (or more) very easily. However, if you double it, make two circles, if you triple, make three. Since these scones freeze well, it is a great way to freeze fruit for later.

Try using frozen fruit. Let it thaw in the fridge, and drain excess water before using. If the fruit is added frozen, be sure to add some cooking time.

Try a mix of fruit in one scone recipe. Blackberry peach is my favorite.

Try pumpkin spice scones with marmalade. Reduce the butter to 2 Tbs, add 1 tsp cinnamon, ½ tsp ground ginger and a pinch of ground cloves. Use 1 Tbs milk, but put in ¼ C pumpkin (or other winter squash) baked and mashed. If you have some extra left over from Sweet & Spicy Squash Soup (see page 108), it would work great here.

Try savory scones. Make two smaller circles and make smaller scones. Use only 1 tsp of sugar, take out the fruit then try tomatoes and basil and/or oregano and Parmesan. Try cheddar cheese and pepper, or jalapeño and/or bacon. Try fennel and sweet onion. Make up your own!

APPLESAUCE ❧

MAKES ABOUT 4 C

8 APPLES

1 C WATER

½ TSP SALT

FOR SPICED APPLESAUCE:

4 CLOVES

4 ALLSPICE BERRIES

2 CINNAMON STICKS
OR 2 TBS GROUND CINNAMON

SOUP POT

KNIFE

CUTTING BOARD

MEASURING SPOONS

WOOD OR PLASTIC SPOON

COLANDER OR SIEVE

SOFT SPATULA

ZIP-TOP BAGS
OR FREEZABLE CONTAINERS

Any apples work, but the best sauce comes from extra juicy, just picked, "new crop" apples. It may seem silly to make what is so easily bought, but the taste will convince you it is worth the effort once in a while . . . or maybe more often. Either stick to the small recipe, or go big. Get together with friends and produce quarts of the stuff — freezing or canning for lunches well into the fall (or winter). Choose a variety with a sweet (rather than tart) apple flavor. Ask for advice if you aren't sure. Growers are happy to share what they know.

PREP TOGETHER. Cut the apples into quarters. For easier straining later, cut out the cores. (If you have a food mill, throw in everything.) Leave the skins on. The extra pectin will make for a richer sauce. Place the apples in the soup pot. (For spiced applesauce, also add the cinnamon sticks, whole cloves, and allspice berries.)

COOK! Pour in the 1 C water and salt, cover and place over high heat for 10 minutes. Turn down the heat to medium-low. Stir the apples occasionally for about 20 minutes or until the apple flesh turns mushy (squash the apple pieces with the back of the spoon as they soften).

Place the colander or sieve over a large bowl. Spoon the softened apples into the colander or sieve. Use the spatula to push the sauce through the holes. Remove the peels and whole spices. (If you have a food mill, spoon the apple in, and turn the crank to separate the yummy from the yucky.)

Give the pot a cursory rinse, and return the applesauce to it. Stir in the 2 Tbs of cinnamon. Cook at a high simmer or low boil to steam off excess water and thicken up the sauce. As the sauce approaches the thickness you want, taste and add more spices if it needs it.

For fun, add some red-hots; they give the sauce a fun pinky-red color. As soon as it is delectable, ladle ½ to 2 cup portions into zip-top bags or snap top containers. Cool and refrigerate or freeze for future consumption.

Applesauce is a great thing to use as your first canning project. It takes an effort to make applesauce "wrong," and since it is already a high sugar and high acid food it can be canned using the simplest methods and no special equipment beyond canning jars, rings and lids, and a big pot. If you decide to do it again with lots of fruit, you may spring for a few things to make it easier.

For terse instructions, go to Ball's website: (*http://www.freshpreserving.com*), or the National Center for Home Food Preservation (*http://nchfp.uga.edu/*). Search for applesauce. Or get the *Ball Blue Book® Guide to Preserving*. Or look through any one of the several blogs out there that show step-by-step instructions.

VARIATIONS. Try cooking the applesauce down until it turns into a cinnamon colored, thick, spreadable, apple butter. Add a few Tbs of sugar to make it glossy and deepen the flavor. Use as you would jam or jelly.

Try peeling the apples along with coring them. Then there is no need to strain. A hand blender, or pressing it through a colander, will still make the applesauce smoother.

Try using a Crockpot. Peel and core the apples, put all the ingredients into a Crockpot, set on high for an hour or two, and squash the apples with the back of a spoon. Dry off the lid, turn down to low for 4 to 6 hours more.

To thicken the sauce more, occasionally take off the lid and dry off the condensation. No worries about burning, and this applesauce can be made while you sleep. Store as above.

Try making pear sauce the same way. Or go with half apples, half pears. Or try mixing in peaches, plums, or other fruits. Try sage or rosemary applesauce by cooking with a handful of sage leaves or a few rosemary twigs. Remove these before serving with pork chops or roast, sausage, or Zucchini Potato Pancakes (see page 100).

SMOOTHIES ꙮ

1 C FRUIT MAKES
1 LARGE OR 2 SMALL SERVINGS

An excellent breakfast, snack or frosty treat, and a great way to get fruit for the day when things get busy, busy, busy! It's even faster when you make these with frozen fruit — no ice cubes needed.

1 C FROZEN FRUIT

1 LARGE SPOONFUL YOGURT

½ C JUICE OF YOUR CHOICE

PREP TOGETHER. As fruit starts rolling in during the summer, faster than you can eat it, prep some for freezing. Give it a good rinse, peel anything with a significant skin (like peaches or melons) and cut into large bite-sized pieces, cutting out any inedible parts like cores, stems, or seeds. Pit cherries before freezing. Berries can be left whole.

CUTTING BOARD

SHARP KNIFE

BLENDER

LARGE SPOON

Spread out the prepared fruit on a baking sheet or the largest pan that fits flat in the freezer. After the fruit has frozen solid, store it in a zip top bag with the air squeezed out.

COOK! In a blender, add two handfuls of frozen fruit, a heaping spoonful of yogurt or silken tofu, and pour the juice into the blender jar until it comes up to the top of the frozen fruit. Place the lid on the blender. Start blending at a lower speed. Then turn up the power and blend until smooth.

For an even faster smoothie in the morning, measure out about 2 C of frozen fruit, and leave it in the fridge overnight. Then you'll be ready to throw everything in the blender even while half-asleep.

VARIATIONS. It is hard to go wrong, and combinations of whatever fruit you have on hand is usually what works best. Using a combination of fresh and frozen fruit is a great option as well. Feel free to get adventurous by adding more savory flavors, like cucumber and leafy greens. Learn what you like and makes you feel good.

SAVORY FRUIT: THE ONES WE USE AS VEGETABLES

CUCUMBERS, ZUCCHINI, & SUMMER SQUASH

PURCHASING. This is easy. All of these are ready to eat as soon as they appear. There is no "ripening." They are ready to eat from the time they are the size of your thumb and still have a blossom on their end all the way up to about the size of your forearm.

As long as they are firm and cool, have no soft spots, and seem heavy for their size, they should be fine.

Watch out for the baseball bat size squash. They can get tough, woody, bitter, and have air pockets inside.

STORAGE. Keep them cool. Local produce specimens are often not waxed and will lose water in the fridge, so keep them bagged. They will also keep for a few days in a very cool corner of your house. Try not to keep them over a week, or they will start to wilt or worse.

To freeze summer squash and zucchini, grate it, squeeze out any excess water, and store in a zip-top bag with all the air squeezed out. Zucchini pancakes, breads, and muffins are a snap from here. Unless you are making granita, cucumbers do not freeze well.

TOMATOES

PURCHASING. Ripe tomatoes are firm, and have a sharp smell. Under-ripe is fine; in a cool spot, place tomatoes stem side down in a single layer in a paper bag or cardboard box, and they will ripen. Keep an eye out for ones that decide to rot, and remove them immediately.

STORAGE. Please try not to refrigerate raw tomatoes. Only buy what you will eat or cook in a short amount of time. Tomatoes for later should be bought under-ripe. Once tomatoes are cooked, cool them as much as you want.

Note: Tomatoes contain flavor compounds that turn off, or lose all their flavor, when the picked tomato is stored below 55°F.

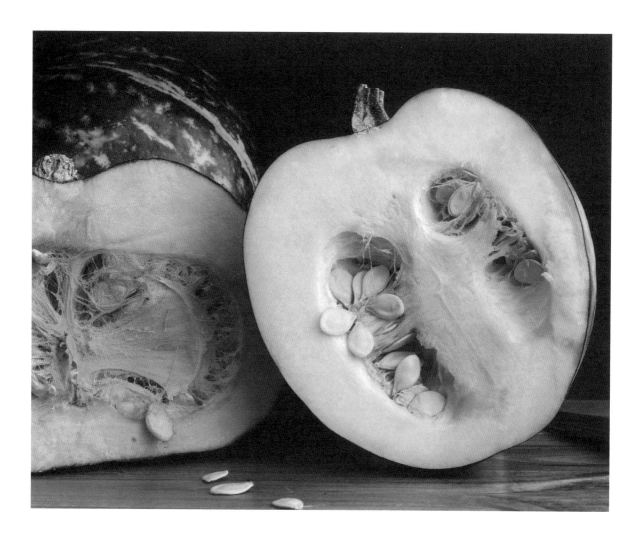

HARD/WINTER SQUASH

PURCHASING.   Look for squash that have a hard, dry stem, feel heavy for their size, and sound hollow when gently, but firmly thumped.

STORAGE.   When left whole, and stored in a very dry, dark, and cool (but not freezing cold) place, like a cellar, they can keep for months. To do this, remove any dirt, then wipe with a dilute bleach solution of ½ tsp bleach in 6 C water. Let them dry and put them away. This discourages the growth of biological bad guys that encourage rot. They also store well when baked in slices or chunks until tender and then frozen. Lay the chunks out in a single layer on a flat pan until solid, then seal in a zip-top bag with the air squeezed out. Then, take out what you need for soups, risotto, baking, and the occasional clever salad.

A FEW BITES OF TOMATO ℰ

MAKES ABOUT ½ C

A HANDFUL OF TOMATOES
....
TASTY OLIVE OIL
....
BALSAMIC VINEGAR
....
SALT & PEPPER TO TASTE
....
BASIL OR OTHER HERBS (OPTIONAL)
....

CUTTING BOARD
....
SHARP KNIFE (KID KNIFE – OPTIONAL)
....
MIXING BOWL
....
SPOON
....

Many tomatoes from farms and farmers markets never even make it home. Often, just a few bites are left. Here's one idea for using them up. Everybody gets a little taste at the beginning of a meal, a nice snack, or a tasty relish maybe with a little toast, or crackers, or a spoon.

PREP TOGETHER. Give the tomatoes a gentle rinse, pull off the stems, and cut into small, bite size pieces (or just cut small tomatoes in half). For every handful of tomatoes, add about 1 tsp of olive oil and ¼ tsp of vinegar. Gently add salt and pepper until it tastes just right.

If you end up eating everything in the process of getting it just right, you are on the right track.

VARIATIONS. Try using green or under-ripe tomatoes, but use more vinegar (try a sharper one), less oil, and some onions to make a fresh relish. Try adding finely chopped garlic (and/or onions) and plenty of herbs for a savory (rather than hot) salsa. Try it on a sandwich with a creamy or soft cheese (mozzarella, ricotta, goat cheese). Try in a sandwich of something savory or peppery (pastrami, roast beef, roasted eggplant, grilled mushroom).

TOASTED TOMATO SANDWICH

MAKE 1 – 2 SANDWICHES PER PERSON

RIPE TOMATOES – ANY SIZE OR COLOR
....
BREAD

CHEDDAR OR MOZZARELLA CHEESE
....

TOASTER OVEN OR
BAKING SHEET & AN OVEN BROILER
....
CUTTING BOARD
....
SHARP KNIFE (KID KNIFE – OPTIONAL)
....
CHEESE GRATER
....

Tomatoes love heat and hate the fridge. This is the perfect quick meal all through tomato season. Make this when you want to enjoy tomato flavor at its peak and then get back outside.

PREP TOGETHER. Cut small tomatoes into halves or quarters, and slice larger tomatoes. Grate or slice cheese, enough cheese for all the sandwiches you want to make. Or use a soft, spreadable cheese.

COOK! If you are making lots of sandwiches or quesadillas, place the bread on the baking sheets now. If you only making 1 or 2, put the bread on a plate. Place or spread the cheese on the bread, place the tomato on top. Broil to toast the bread, melt the cheese, and sizzle the tomato a little. Eat the sandwich open-faced or fold it over as it comes out of the oven.

VARIATIONS. Try making this on large crackers. Try adding other flavors to the sandwich. Try a little salt and pepper on the tomato, or a seasoned salt. Try adding some herbs.

Try adding sliced onions — green onions, purple, sweet, and so on. Try some sautéed onions, garlic scapes or chutes, or other grilled veggies.

Try adding a little mustard under the cheese, or hot sauce or salsa over the top. Try spreading tuna salad on the bread, then top with tomatoes and cheese for the most divine tuna-melt ever.

Try the next recipe in this book if you are ready for a bit of a challenge and huge rewards.

GRILLED CHEESE & TOMATO SANDWICH ∾

This is NOT the same at all as a toasted cheese sandwich. It requires more equipment and effort, but oh, it is worth it. Crispy fried bread on the outside, and melted cheese surrounding juicy savory tomatoes makes the end of tomato season, and the nice summer weather, a little less painful.

PREP TOGETHER. Cut small tomatoes into halves or quarters, and slice larger tomatoes. Grate or slice cheese, enough cheese for all the sandwiches you want to make. A large loose handful of grated cheese per sandwich is about right.

COOK! Sprinkle half the cheese on one slice of bread, spread out a single layer of tomato, then sprinkle on the rest of the cheese. Top with the other piece of bread. Spread softened butter on the outside of the bread, or use a pastry brush to apply a thin coating of oil. Heat your sauté pan over medium heat with a pat of butter or a splash of oil. A small piece of tomato will sizzle in the butter or oil when the pan is hot.

Place the sandwich in the hot pan. Cover with the lid for 2 to 3 minutes. Check to see if the bread is golden brown and crunchy. If it is, flip! If not quite yet, keep an eye on it, and flip when it gets there. Clap the lid on for another 2 to 3 minutes (this helps keep the heat in and melt the cheese). Check the second side for crispiness, and the inside for meltiness. If the bread is toasting too fast, turn the heat down!

When you've reached crispy outside and melted insides, remove and serve hot — maybe with a sour pickle or cucumbers and some radishes from The Radish Problem (see page 144).

VARIATIONS. Try adding some cured meat, like bacon, ham, salami, or pastrami. Try sprinkling your tomatoes with Worcestershire sauce before they go in the sandwich. Try adding some onions for a savory punch.

Check your fridge. Is there something in there that would be good with grilled cheese and tomatoes?

Try this with the Sweet & Spicy Butternut Squash Soup (see page 108).

MAKE 1 – 2 SANDWICHES PER PERSON

RIPE TOMATOES – ANY SIZE OR COLOR

2 SLICES OF BREAD PER SANDWICH

CHEDDAR, MOZZARELLA OR OTHER MELTABLE CHEESE

SOFTENED BUTTER OR OIL

CUTTING BOARD

SHARP KNIFE (KID KNIFE OPTIONAL)

CHEESE GRATER

BUTTER KNIFE

PASTRY BRUSH (OPTIONAL)

SAUTÉ PAN & LID

FLIPPING SPATULA

OVEN ROASTED SUMMER SQUASH

SERVES 2 – 4

2 – 4 MEDIUM SUMMER SQUASH

2 TSP OIL

SALT & PEPPER TO TASTE

PARMESAN CHEESE (OPTIONAL)

KNIFE (KID KNIFE – OPTIONAL)

CUTTING BOARD

BAKING PAN

MEASURING SPOONS

SPOON (OPTIONAL)

CHEESE GRATER (OPTIONAL)

Summer squash is a very watery specimen. Roasting to evaporate most of the water — until some edges get brown and crispy — enhances this subtle vegetable . . . err, fruit and brings out the most flavor. The extra perks include: it uses up a bunch of summer squash at once, the leftovers make a mean quesadilla the next day, and once in the oven it requires no fussing.

PREP TOGETHER. Rub the squash under running water to remove the rough feeling from the squash skin (these are little guard hairs). Use the knife to trim the ends off the squash. Cut the squash into finger-width slices or, slice the long way to make two boats, and scrape out the seeds with a spoon. (Grate a handful of cheese — optional.)

COOK! Heat the oven to 425°F. Toss the squash on the baking pan with the oil, salt, and pepper. If you have boats, place them skin side down. Bake the squash for about 25 to 35 minutes. If you have small pieces, give the pan a shake at about 20 minutes, and check the smallest pieces to see if they are wilted and starting to get brown edges.

If you would like a little cheese on the squash, sprinkle it on, return the pan to the oven for about 5 minutes or until the cheese has melted and most of the pieces have some brown, crispy edges. If it needs a little more oomph, sprinkle on a bit of Worcestershire sauce to enhance the flavor.

VARIATIONS. Add some extra flavor to the summer squash. Try seasoned salt in place of the salt and pepper. Try adding a little vinegar or vinaigrette dressing when it comes out of the oven. Try baking some onions (green or regular) with the squash. Add herbs near the end — alone or with cheese.

Try basil, cilantro, oregano, dill, parsley, summer savory, mint, or a mixture of whatever you have on hand.

SUBSTITUTIONS...

Summer squash options:
zucchini
yellow
crook neck
patty pan

Cheeses:
feta cheese
ricotta salata
Romano cheese
Iberico cheese
check the Farmer's Market

Herbs:
basil
oregano
thyme
marjoram
parsley
dill
cilantro
summer savory
a mix

SUMMER SQUASH, CABBAGE & SWEET ONION SALAD ✑

Make this when you need a salad, but you don't have regular salad ingredients. The lettuce has bolted, everyone has had enough green salads for the moment, or there's just a bunch of summer squash lying around and you aren't sure what to do with it. However you end up deciding to make this, its green, sweet, and pungent flavors come together in surprising ways.

PREP TOGETHER. Cut off the ends of the squash. If it is medium size, cut in half length-wise. Small ones can stay whole. Slice the squash about ¼-inch thick (a bit thinner than your pinky). This can be done with a kid knife or a sharp knife. Toss the squash into a medium bowl with about a ¼ tsp of salt. Set aside. The squash will drain some excess water, which concentrates the flavor.

In the serving bowl (or a small bowl), make the dressing. Stir together the mustard and about 3 Tbs total of acid (vinegar, with or without the citrus juice). Add any herbs, roughly chopped, and a few shakes or grinds of pepper. Taste and adjust, but wait to add salt until the dish is assembled. Slowly pour in the tasty oil while vigorously stirring the vinegar mixture with the fork or whisk. (All the dressing ingredients can also be placed in a small snap top container and shaken.)

Cut the onion in half through the root, peel off the dry layers, and slice as thinly as possible. Stir the onion into the dressing, and let it marinate. This is a good place to stop as all ingredients can be covered and set aside for a few hours, or refrigerated overnight.

COOK! Preheat your sauté pan or grill over medium-high heat. Thinly slice the cabbage, and toss with the marinating onions. Drain excess water from the squash and toss with 1 tsp cooking oil.

Place as many squash pieces on the hot grill or pan that will fit loosely in one layer. This will require two or more batches depending on the amount of squash and the size of the pan or grill. Do not stir the squash. Instead, let it rest in place and develop brown edges or grill marks (2 to 4 minutes). When one side has brown marks, flip it over and cook until brown marks develop on the other side. Place the hot squash directly in the salad, and toss it in. Continue with the rest of the squash.

Serve it as soon as all the squash are cooked for an exciting mix of flavors, textures, and temperatures.

VARIATIONS. Try using regular onions, slice them about finger width, and cook or grill them like the squash. Marinate them in the dressing, and continue with the rest of the recipe.

Try grilling the onions, and slice the squash very thin. Make it translucent if possible. Add the squash raw. No need to drain it.

Try replacing the squash with cucumbers. Try adding tomatoes. Try different combinations of herbs.

SUBSTITUTIONS...

green or purple cabbage
different shapes and color of squash
regular onions, but grill them
cucumbers
add tomatoes

Herbs:
mint & dill
mint & basil
mint & parsley
basil & parsley
chives & dill
make up you own

For more zing in the dressing, add some lemon, lime or orange juice

SEASONAL MINESTRONE SOUP ❧

SERVES 4 – 6

4 C BROTH

2 TBS OIL

2 CLOVES GARLIC

½ C CHOPPED ONION

2 FIST SIZED TOMATOES
OR A 14.5 OZ. CAN

¾ C SMALL PASTA

SALT & PEPPER TO TASTE

5 – 7 C DICED VEGETABLES

CUTTING BOARD

KNIFE

PARING KNIFE (OPTIONAL)

SOUP POT

LONG SPOON OR FLAT SPATULA

SAUCEPAN

CONTAINERS FOR CHOPPED VEGETABLES

MEASURING CUPS

MEASURING SPOONS

VEGETABLE OPTIONS:

1 C LEGUMES

3 C HEARTY LEAVES

2 C SOMETHING SWEET AND CRUNCHY

1 C OTHER VEGETABLES

HANDFUL OF HERBS

Making minestrone used to drive me bonkers. Recipes called for a half cup of eight different vegetables. How do you shop for that? When I started dabbling in gardening, it suddenly made sense. This is the soup to make when only a little of this and a little of that is ready. It is the perfect expression of your local produce in a garlicky, tomato broth.

PREP TOGETHER.   Leave the chicken stock out of it for the moment. Smash, peel, and finely chop the garlic. Cut the onion in half through the root, peel off the dry layers, then chop it into pieces smaller than the top joint of your pinky.

Clean all the vegetables appropriately. Shell the peas or rinse the canned beans. Wash the leaves, and remove tough stems. Cut across the leaves to make inch-wide strips that will be easy to handle with a spoon. If the sweet and crunchy element is tender (green beans, asparagus) cut bigger pieces (as long as your thumb). If it is crunchier (carrots, etc.), dice it into pieces approximately the size of the top joint of your pointer finger. For any other vegetables, trim ends and remove any tough skins. Cut them up into the small pieces as well.

Cut out the tough core of the tomato (the tough, flavorless bit under the stem), and cut the tomatoes into the same small size pieces.

COOK!   Put the four cups of broth in the saucepan, place it over high heat to bring it to a boil. Once it boils, reduce it to a simmer and have it standing by. While the broth is heating up, place the soup pot over medium heat, with the 2 Tbs of oil. Let the pot heat for about 4 minutes or until a small piece of onion sizzles. Add the onion and a pinch of salt, and stir the onion until it starts to soften. Add the garlic, and stir until it is fragrant and starts to turn golden.

Add any hard vegetables (carrots, fennel, potatoes, turnips — anything you judge needs to be well cooked). Continue to stir occasionally over the heat for about 15 minutes.

After the hard vegetables have had time to soften, stir in the tomatoes. Cook another 10 minutes or so or until the tomatoes have released their juices and excess water has cooked off. This will concentrate flavors for a tastier soup.

Finally, add all the other vegetables, including leaves, and the pasta or rice (exception: save out fresh peas until the last second), and pour on the hot broth. Simmer until the pasta and the other vegetables have softened (add fresh peas now). Taste the nearly completed soup. Add any needed salt and pepper.

Chop any fresh herbs. Serve the soup, top with the optional fresh herbs. Enjoy it with something crispy on the side.

VARIATIONS. Try a generous grating of Parmesan or other hard, salty cheese over the top. Try a spoonful of pesto on top to recreate the French Provençal dish, *Soupe de Pistou.* Try adding a small handful of chopped herbs when adding the tomatoes: basil, oregano, thyme, parsley, and marjoram all add something nice.

Try spring minestrone. Use garden peas for the beans (be sure to add at the last second); chard for the leaves; asparagus and chard stems for the crunchy bit; fennel for the other vegetables.

Try summer minestrone. Use sweet onions, but don't cook them down too much; green beans and/or fava beans for the beans; spinach or chard for the leaves; juicy summer carrots and baby turnips for the crunch; use a variety of sweet summer squash for the rest of the vegetables. Make the most of summer's bounty by adding a spicy pepper chopped fine with the tomatoes.

Try fall minestrone. Use shell beans (or maybe canned beans); kale for the leaves (it may need a bit longer simmer in the broth); bigger fall carrots and cauliflower or other crunchy, hearty vegetables; add potatoes; maybe some small peeled cubes of early hard winter squash

Decide on the vegetable mixture based on what is available. The proportions are a starting point; feel free to improvise. Generally, a minestrone has a bean element, a leaf element, a crunchy or firm element, and a soft element. Fill these roles as the season in your region provides.

SUBSTITUTIONS...

Legumes:
fresh peas
canned beans
fava beans
edamame

Hearty leaves:
kale, chard, collards, cabbage, Brussels sprouts?, something exotic?
something sweet & crunchy:
green beans, asparagus, celery, carrots, chard stems? baby turnips?

Other vegetables:
zucchini
summer squash
cauliflower
fennel
potatoes

Herbs:
basil, oregano, thyme, parsley, marjoram, chives, dill

Pasta options:
shells, broken spaghetti, tiny macaroni, melon seed pasta
leftover rice, other leftover cooked grains.

ZUCCHINI PANCAKES TWO WAYS

3 C ZUCCHINI MAKES
ABOUT 12 PANCAKES

FOR EVERY 3 C GRATED ZUCCHINI:

½ AN ONION – ALSO GRATED

½ C CHICK PEA OR WHEAT FLOUR

1 EGG

SALT & PEPPER

HANDFUL OF HERBS (OPTIONAL)

COOKING OIL – AMOUNT VARIES BY
METHOD

SHARP KNIFE

CUTTING BOARD

MIXING BOWL

FOOD PROCESSOR OR OTHER GRATER

SALAD SPINNER OR COLANDER

SEVERAL KITCHEN TOWELS

MEASURING CUPS

MEASURING SPOONS

MIXING SPOON OR RUBBER SPATULA

FLIPPING SPATULA

SAUTÉ PAN

OR

HEAVY POT 4 – 8 INCHES HIGH

This is the first recipe that made me feel like I didn't have enough zucchini. So this is a great one for the height of zucchini season. This versatile recipe is proportional, so it can be easily expanded for the occasional zucchini crisis, and it has lots of options for freezing along the way.

PREP TOGETHER With the large knife, chop the large zucchini into manageable-sized pieces. If the seeds look particularly spongy and dry, use a metal spoon to scoop them out. Grate the zucchini, and place the result in a salad spinner or colander for the first round of draining. Grate all the zucchini; you can freeze any extra.

When it is all grated, spread out a thin layer of zucchini over a kitchen towel, roll it up, and squeeze mercilessly to get out extra water. You may need to do this in several batches depending on the amount of zucchini.

Measure out the 3 cups of zucchini. Put the rest in a zip-top bag, squeeze out the air, label, and stash in the freezer. Grate the onion. Use clean hands to stir these together, add in the flour, egg, salt, and pepper (herbs are optional). Combine until just mixed.

COOK! Flat Pancake Way: Place a griddle or sauté pan over medium-high heat. Give it a light coating of oil. After about 3 or 4 minutes, when a bit of the pancake batter sizzles raucously on the surface, it is hot enough. Spoon batter onto the griddle to make pancakes the size you want.

Press down on the pancakes with the flipping spatula to flatten them out. After a minute or two, peek and see if the bottom is browning nicely. If yes, flip! If no, wait until it has, then flip. Cook until the edges are nice and crispy. Adjust the heat if you feel the pancakes are cooking too quickly or slowly. Set aside on a cooling rack or paper towels. Eat the first one as hot as you can with some pepper.

Fried Pancake Way: Heat ¼- to ½-inch of oil in a Dutch oven or other high-sided, heavy pot to 350° F, or until a dot of batter sizzles merrily and cooks by the time you count to ten. (The oil should be well below the smoke point. If you see smoke, turn the heat off or way down immediately, then turn it back up gradually.)

Note: If you have never deep-fried or pan fried before, please take these basic precautions: (1) Have a large lid handy in case you need to smother a flame. (2) Never EVER use water in flaming oil.

Fry zucchini pancake patties that are about 1 to 2 heaping tablespoons in size. Only cook 3 or 4 at a time so the oil doesn't cool down too much. Each pancake will take about 3 or 4 minutes on each side to get golden brown on the outside with crispy edges, and soft and wonderful on the inside. The eating of several test pancakes may be required. Drain on a cooling rack over paper towels.

For both ways, when you get the timing down, cook all the rest of the pancakes. Keep these warm in an oven that has been heated to 250°F and turned off. Don't cover them, or they will get soggy. Extras can be refrigerated or frozen.

Reheat on a rack at 350°F or in a toaster oven for 5 to 10 minutes, or until they regain their crispy edges. Turn the heat off or way down if you see smoke.

Never leave hot oil unattended while it is on the heat. If you don't already have a kitchen fire extinguisher, it is time to get one, and don't store it above the stove. The fire extinguisher is not just for frying. But, that said, don't be afraid of the fry. It is worth learning how to do.

Also note that many starchy flours work. I started with wheat, but have come to favor chick pea (garbanzo). Rice and potato flours are also good options.

SUBSTITUTIONS...

Which herbs go best with zucchini?
dill – and lots of it.
basil
parsley
thyme
oregano
chives

Makes an excellent summer breakfast. Try toasted with soft cheese.

VARIATIONS. Try replacing 1 C of zucchini with 1 C grated potato. It makes a different but equally tasty pancake. Try yellow summer squash if that is what you have, they are interchangeable with zucchini. Try dill-zucchini pancakes or fritters. They are classic Middle Eastern fare. Try them with hummus and yogurt.

Try grating in some jalapeño peppers and using the pancakes under huevos rancheros instead of tortillas. (A stack of refried beans, fried egg, and salsa).

Try making tiny ones and serving with salty olives or cured meat for appetizers. Try a toasted one in the morning with cottage cheese or other soft, fresh cheese as a grown up replacement for the toaster waffle.

SESAME SOY ZUCCHINI

Make this when you have to do something with the zucchini before it goes bad, but you don't have much time or can't face anymore just now. This will give you that time. The zucchini gets better when it has time to marinate for a few days, and drain away excess water. Oh, and it'll still work for dinner tonight.

PREP TOGETHER. Rinse the zucchini and trim off the ends. Cut in half, or quarters so all the seeds are exposed. With the metal spoon, gently scoop out the seeds. Cut the zucchini into slices pinky width or thinner (they will shrink). Place the pieces in the container or zip-top bag. Add the soy sauce and sesame oil, adjusting amounts so all the pieces will be coated, but not swimming.

Close the container tightly, so it won't leak. Shake vigorously. Place it in the refrigerator, turning it when you remember over the next 2 to 5 days.

COOK! When you are in need of a vegetable for a meal, take out this zucchini. Remove it from the marinade. There will be more liquid and less zucchini than you started with. Excess water from the zucchini has drained out, leaving it much tastier.

Cook this zucchini over a grill if you are able. If not, sauté in a pan heated up over medium-high heat with maybe 1 tsp of oil in the bottom. In any case, cook it until nice brown marks show up on the zucchini.

Alternately, drape the zucchini on a rack over a drip pan at 425°F for about 15 minutes until the edges get a little brown and crispy. Whatever you do, enjoy the unexpected deliciousness of zucchini relegated to the back of the fridge for several days.

1 ZUCCHINI SERVES 2 – 3

AT THE MINIMUM:

1 MEDIUM ZUCCHINI
OR SUMMER SQUASH

2 TBS SOY SAUCE

2 TSP SESAME OIL

SHARP KNIFE

CUTTING BOARD

METAL SPOON

MEASURING SPOONS

SNAP TOP CONTAINER OR ZIP TOP BAG

GRILL OR SAUTÉ PAN

FORK OR TONGS

MEXICAN CHOCOLATE ZUCCHINI BREAD ～

**MAKES 2 9 X 4 LOAVES OR
ABOUT 2 DOZ. REGULAR MUFFINS**

3 C GRATED ZUCCHINI

3½ C FLOUR

½ C COCOA POWDER

1 C (REGULAR) SUGAR

¼ C PACKED BROWN SUGAR

5 TSP BAKING POWDER

1 TBS GROUND CINNAMON

¹/₈ TO ½ TSP CAYENNE PEPPER

½ TSP SALT

1½ C MILK

¼ C OIL

2 TSP VANILLA EXTRACT

2 EGGS

1C CHOCOLATE CHIPS (OPTIONAL)

This was my first "zucchini avalanche" recipe. The classic zucchini bread I was making kept sitting around. I had to do something. This chocolaty treat, with a spicy kick at the end, flew off the plate making room for more, and it is the only way I have ever found to gift zucchini to friends and then keep them as friends. This is for two 9- by 4-inch loaves, or LOTS of muffins — which freeze extremely well.

PREP TOGETHER. Grate the zucchini, lay it out in a thin layer on a kitchen towel, roll it up, and squeeze the water out mercilessly. Do the same thing if thawing previously frozen grated zucchini.

In a large bowl, combine all the dry ingredients (flour, cocoa powder, both sugars, baking powder, cinnamon, cayenne, and salt). Stir gently to combine. Make sure there are no islands or lumps of any one thing. In the small bowl, stir together milk, oil, vanilla, and eggs. Add the zucchini and gently stir in.

Add the wet ingredients to the dry. Use the spoon to fold the dry ingredients over and around the wet. Stir until just combined. Last, quickly, but gently, stir in the optional chocolate pieces.

COOK! Preheat the oven to 350° F. Use a paper towel with a little oil poured on it to grease the pans. Or line muffin tins with cupcake papers. Pour or spoon the batter up to ²/₃ full into desired baking vessel (pan, muffin tin). Place the bread on the center rack of the oven. Bake until done.

Done means muffins spring back at a light finger poke. For bread, check the center with a toothpick. It should come out clean or a

little crumby. Not gooey. For tiny muffins, about 12 minutes; for regular sized muffins, about 22 minutes; for giant muffins, try 35 to 45 minutes.

For the larger loaf pans, check at an hour, though 1 hour plus 10 to 15 minutes is normal. Really, bake this in whatever pan you have, and it is done when the center is moist and crumby and no longer gooey.

Let the bread cool at least 5 minutes before removing it from the pan or tins. Then let it cool the rest of the way on a rack.

To freeze, cool the bread completely. Wrap in plastic wrap, then heavy-duty foil or freezer paper. Label and freeze for 3 to 4 months. Or place in a freezer bag, squeeze out excess air. Label and freeze for 3 to 4 months. (Sliced loaves and muffins can be removed a serving at a time).

VARIATIONS. This can be converted to classic zucchini bread by replacing the cocoa powder with ½ C of flour, and replacing the cinnamon and cayenne with 1 tsp lemon zest or ½ tsp lemon extract, 2 tsp cinnamon and ¼ tsp nutmeg.

For optional frosting, as if this isn't good enough on it's own, you can make a quick topping of softened cream cheese or mild goat cheese. Stir in a little milk to make it creamy. Add orange zest, ginger, and honey or sugar (maybe a little salt). Use your own taste buds to find the most delicious combination.

WARNING: This frosting pushes the bread the rest of the way over to cake.

9 X 4 INCH LOAF PANS OR MUFFIN TINS

CUPCAKE PAPERS (OPTIONAL)

TOOTHPICK

LARGE BOWL

SMALL BOWL

FOOD PROCESSOR

MEASURING CUPS

MEASURING SPOONS

FORK/WHISK

STIRRING SPOON

KITCHEN TOWELS

PAPER TOWELS

SUBSTITUTIONS...

Try a disk of Mexican hot chocolate hammered into little chunks in place of the chocolate chips.

No food processor? Use your regular grater.

BAKED DELICATA WINTER SQUASH ❧

1 SQUASH SERVES 2

FOR 1 SQUASH:

1 TBS BROWN SUGAR

1 TBS BUTTER

PINCH OF SALT

UP TO ½ C WATER

SHARP KNIFE (YOUR HEAVIEST ONE)

CUTTING BOARD

METAL SPOON

MEASURING SPOONS

BAKING PAN

FORK

SMALL BOWL

VEGETABLE PEELER (OPTIONAL)

Delicata is a dainty "starter" squash. The sweet dense flesh is similar in texture to a sweet potato, and can be used in similar ways. Once you feel comfortable with crowd friendly, adorable squash, you can start tackling the big guys. Bonus: This is really a master recipe for all winter squashes. Larger squashes will take longer. Do try different varieties to find your favorite texture and flavor.

PREP TOGETHER. Optionally, peel off a little patch to create a flat spot on the squash so it is more stable on the cutting board. With firm steady pressure, cut the squash in half the long way, so it looks like 2 boats.

Use the metal spoon to scrape out and discard the strings and seeds. Use a fork to squish together the butter and brown sugar in the small bowl, and be sure to add the pinch of salt. Set this aside until the squash is half cooked.

COOK! Heat the oven to 425°F. Place the squash so the yellow inside is face down in the shallow pan. Pour in enough water so there is just a shallow pool in the bottom of the pan (no more than ¼-inch deep). Cook the squash for 25 minutes. Remove the pan from the oven.

Turn the squash face up, and divide the butter and brown sugar mixture between the squash halves. Place the squash back in the oven for about 15 more minutes or until the squash is fork tender, the butter is melted, and the sugar has begun to bubble a little. If the squash gets a little crusty on the edges, that's even better.

This same thing can be done with any other dense fleshed squash. Kabocha and many varieties of acorn squash and small or pie-pumpkins are great this way. When pondering what variety to try next, ask. Or a good rule of thumb is larger squash varieties tend to be stringier, smaller varieties tend to be denser and sweeter. With the larger varieties, cut the squash into single serving wedges to make them easier to handle and shorten the cooking time.

VARIATIONS. Try cutting the squash into even smaller wedges, tossing them with oil and salt (similar to Herb Roasted Potatoes on page 131). Bake them until they have crispy edges. Add them hot to a Big Green Salad (see page 8) for a totally different twist.

Try different spices or herbs in the butter instead of sugar for a more savory approach. Garlic and paprika butter is delicious.

Try taking squashes back to their South and Central American roots by tossing roasted squash wedges with toasted green pumpkin seeds (pepitas), fresh cheese, and chopped onions and oregano.

SWEET & SPICY BUTTERNUT SQUASH SOUP ❧

SERVES 8 (OR 4 TWICE)

ABOUT 2 LBS. BUTTERNUT SQUASH

OIL

4 C BROTH

6 GARLIC CLOVES

2 TBS GROUND GINGER

1 ONION

2 TSP SALT – OR MORE TO TASTE

1/8 TSP CAYENNE PEPPER

1/4 TSP CARDAMOM

1/2 TSP CINNAMON

2 TBS HONEY

2 C MILK

CUTTING BOARD

SHARP KNIFE

BAKING SHEET

LARGE POT

VEGETABLE PEELER

METAL SPOON

MEASURING CUPS

MEASURING SPOONS

BLENDER/HAND BLENDER

LARGE STIRRING SPOON

I came up with this soup in reaction to a variety of bland, sad pumpkin soups. Squash alone has a vague sweet and earthy flavor making it a blank canvas for building your own flavors. That means you can really make this soup with any sweet, dense (not stringy) fleshed pumpkin, kabocha or other winter squash. And you can personalize it with your own bold spice combinations.

PREP TOGETHER. Preheat the oven 425°F. Cut 2 pounds of squash into pieces that will be easy to hold while peeling off the skin. Scoop out the seeds with the metal spoon, and use a knife or vegetable peeler to remove the hard skin.

Cut the peeled squash into approximately 2-inch pieces. Place the squash pieces on the baking sheet, toss with just enough oil to coat. Roast the squash in the oven for 20 minutes, or until the pieces are fork tender. Set aside to cool.

While the squash is baking, slice the onion through the root end, peel off the outer dry layers, then slice and chop it into small pieces. Smash, peel and finely chop the garlic. (If you are using fresh ginger, use the vegetable peeler to remove the dry skin from the ginger, and finely chop it.) Measure out the dry spices.

Note: This soup can be made in stages. The squash can be frozen after it is baked, and the soup can be made later. Or bake a whole bunch of squash, use 2 pounds for the recipe and save the rest for something else. Or make a whole bunch of soup, but only finish with milk the part you want to eat right away, and freeze the rest for later.

COOK! Place the soup pot over medium-high heat. Add about 1 Tbs oil to coat the bottom. The pot will be ready in 3 to 4 minutes, or when a small piece of onion sizzles in the oil.

Add the onions to the oil with a pinch of salt. Stir the onions until they start to get translucent, about 5 minutes. Add the garlic and ginger. Stir until they are fragrant. Add the dry spices, and stir well. When the kitchen smells nice and spicy, add the cooked squash, half the stock, and the honey. Stir until all the ingredients are evenly distributed, and heated through.

Time to blend. Use a hand blender, or ladle parts of the soup into a traditional blender, process until the soup is as smooth as you want it to be. Use the rest of the stock to smooth out the soup. If you prefer very smooth soup, pour the blended soup through a sieve. If you are without a blender, smash the squash with a spoon, then use a rubber spatula to squish the soup through a sieve or a colander.

To finish the soup, add the 2 C of milk and check for salt and spice. There's no hurry with soup. Take the time to make it right.

VARIATIONS. Try with cheesy garlic toast for a spectacular cold weather lunch. Try with a sprinkle of pumpkin seeds (pepitas) on top, and/or a little sour cream or plain yogurt. Try adding cooked chicken or sausage at the end for an even heartier soup.

Try a different spice mix. Leave out the original spices. Replace them with 1 to 2 tsp of curry powder (or 1 Tbs curry paste). Be sure to use coconut milk at the end, and maybe a few splashes of fish sauce. Serve with rice, chicken satay, or grilled shrimp.

Try an herb flavored soup. Leave out the honey, replace the cayenne pepper with ¼ tsp red pepper flakes, and replace the spices with 2 bay leaves, a tsp of dried thyme and a tsp of oregano. Or switch out the thyme for rosemary or sage. Or use fresh herbs instead.

SUBSTITUTIONS...

Fresh ginger (minced).

Which broth? Chicken and vegetable are both good.

No dairy for you?
coconut milk (my favorite)
rice milk
soy milk
almond milk
or just more broth.

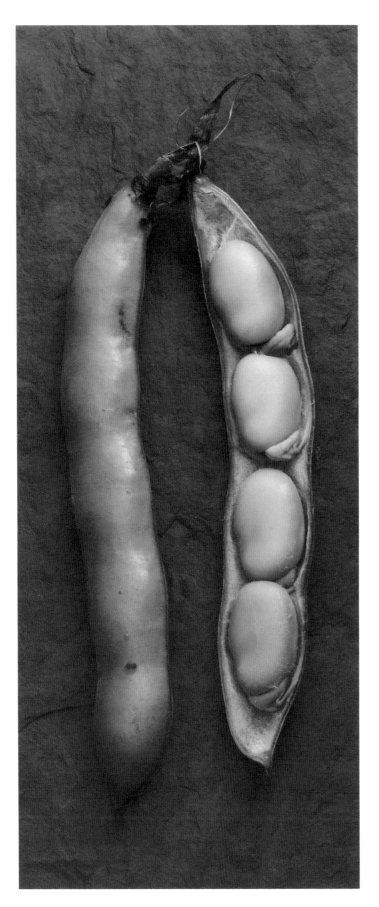

seeds

oven roasted green beans

beans, bacon & summer savory

minty peas with butter

grilled fava beans

fava beans in garlicky dressing

quickest sweet corn

grilled corn on the cob

roasted pumpkin seeds

eas, beans (in and out of the shell), corn, and pumpkin seeds (pepitas); as the start of a new plant, seeds are packed with nutrition and flavor. As fresh foods, they have a limited tasty life. The sweetness we love is trying to turn into less tasty, more stable starch. So get these goodies from plant to table as quickly as you can.

GREEN BEANS & PEA PODS

These are eatable shells and seeds.

PURCHASING. Look for vibrant green and a firm, snappy feel. Stay away from anything dry, limp, yellowy-brown, slimy, or too swollen. (It's too old; the seeds inside have made the shell tough.) Some beans come in yellow and purple varieties too. Don't worry, it's easy to pick out the tasty looking ones in those colors too.

STORAGE. Wrap them up unwashed in a barely damp kitchen towel or a produce bag, and use them soon for the sweetest and greenest flavors.

GARDEN PEAS/ENGLISH PEAS

PURCHASING. Look for well swollen pea pods that are still firm and green. Yellow or limp pods

mean the peas are headed towards starchy and may have started to dry out a bit.

STORAGE. Try to use them that day (they can sit out on the counter), or wrap them up in a produce bag or barely damp kitchen towel, and keep them cool in the fridge to slow down the march to starchiness, for a day or three.

SHELLING BEANS

These are mainly Fava beans, but more varieties may appear at your market any day now. These are "old world" beans that have a pod and then an inedible skin around each bean that also needs to be peeled off. Soybeans (edamame) and garbanzo beans (chickpeas) fall into this category as well.

PURCHASING. Blemished pods are fine as long as they are overall plump and green. The beans you want are well protected inside. Stay away from pods that are starting to dry out or have slimy spots. These have gone too far.

STORAGE. Wrapped up in the fridge, the pods will keep for at least a week. But once you start removing the beans from the pods and the fussy green skins, keep at it, and use them pretty quickly.

OVEN ROASTED GREEN BEANS ✑

SERVES 2 – 4

1 LB GREEN BEANS

2 TSP OIL

SALT

BAKING SHEET

COLANDER

STIRRING SPATULA

Make these with the firm, crunchy beans at the height of summer. You will be amazed by they way they smell, taste, and disappear. These beans don't need fussing over, and they bring new flavors and textures to the plate. These are a must if you've had it with limp, bland green beans.

PREP TOGETHER.   Give the beans a good bath in plenty of water. Move the beans to a colander, and let them drain. Take the beans out one by one. Break off the stem end. Most beans are now "stringless," so there is no tough string across the top of the bean to pull off. But if a string is connected from the end, pull it off. It is not good to eat. The tiny pointy end where the flower used to be can be left on.

Discard any stems and leaves. The beans can also be lined up, and the stem ends chopped off in a group. Place the cleaned beans on the baking sheet.

COOK!   Heat the oven to 425°F. Drizzle the oil over the beans, and sprinkle on about 1 tsp salt. Mix thoroughly with clean hands. Place in the oven for 12 to 25 minutes. (Different size and age beans have very different cooking times). After 10 minutes, shake and stir the beans. If some are starting to get a little brown on the bottom, then they are almost done. If there is no browning check again in 2 or 3 minutes.

When the beans get a little brown on their bottoms, remove them from the oven, and move into a serving bowl. Taste test for salt. If they need more, give a little sprinkle now. Serve right away!

Note: Pod beans can be divided into New World Beans (Western Hemisphere), and Old World Beans (Eastern Hemisphere), more or less. Green beans and most of the ones where you eat the pod, seeds, and the fine skin surrounding them are New World Beans. Beans where you have to shell them, and remove a tough skin are usually Old World beans. Look for New World beans in Purple, Rattlesnake, Wax, and Yellow varieties, and use any in this recipe.

VARIATIONS.   Try glazing the beans. After the first stir and check, stir the beans with a mixture of 1 Tbs balsamic vinegar and 1 Tbs brown sugar per pound of beans.

Try adding whole peeled garlic cloves or large slices of sweet onion to the beans. This is especially good with the balsamic and brown sugar glaze and packs well as a cold picnic salad.

Try some Asian flavors. Use sesame oil, and soy sauce, then sprinkle with sesame seeds. Try oyster sauce as a glaze.

Try some Mediterranean flavors. Stir chopped tomato, finely chopped garlic and basil or oregano into the beans right when they come out of the oven. Maybe a squeeze of lemon too.

Try stirring in chopped almonds, hazelnuts, pecans, pine nuts, or pumpkin seeds during the last 5 minutes of cooking. (No earlier, or they might burn.)

Try stirring in some herbs either in the last 5 minutes of cooking, or when you take them out of the oven. Basil, parsley, dill, oregano, chives and savory are all very nice. So are some others I've accidentally left out.

BEANS, BACON & SUMMER SAVORY ᔥ

SERVES 2 – 4

1 LB GREEN BEANS

1 TSP OIL

2 SLICES OF BACON

1 ONION

SALT & PEPPER

1 OR 2 SPRIGS SUMMER SAVORY

¼ C BROTH

KITCHEN TOWELS

SAUCE PAN & LID

COLANDER

STIRRING SPATULA

SMALL BOWL

MEASURING SPOONS

KNIFE

CUTTING BOARD

While this recipe is for fresh green beans, it is just as tasty with beans of all sorts and stages. Summer savory has such a history with beans, it is often grown with them in kitchen gardens and is even referred to as "bean herb."

PREP TOGETHER.   Give the green beans a good bath in plenty of water and pat dry. Trim the stem ends off the green beans; either pinch the stem off with your fingers, and pull off any strings, or line up the beans and chop the stem ends off with a knife (most beans are "stringless" these days). The pointy end that used to have the flower on it can be left on.

Chop the beans in half. Set aside. Cut the onion in half through the root end. Peel off any dry outer layers. Lay the halves flat on the cutting board. Make three equally spaced slices from the root end to the top. Then make slices about as wide as your pinky. Gather the chopped onions in a pile and set aside.

Strip the summer savory leaves off their stems and roughly chop. Set aside. Stack the slices of bacon, and cut into thin matchsticks.

COOK!   Pour about a ½-inch (just under the top joint of your pinky) of water into the saucepan. Place the pan, cover on, over high heat and bring the water to a boil. Add a large pinch of salt, and put in the beans. Cover the beans, put the pan back on the heat, and let the beans braise for about 8 minutes or until the beans are no longer squeaky against your teeth when you bite into one (but still has a little crunch and plenty of body).

Pour the beans and water out into the colander in your sink and let them sit to the side. Place the empty pan back on medium high-heat, add the oil and sliced bacon. Cook the bacon until it is crisp. Remove the bacon to a small bowl.

Add in the onion, with another large pinch of salt, and stir it, sizzling, over the medium-high heat, until it turns translucent and gets some brown edges. If the onion edges are getting brown (or black!) while the center is still mostly white, turn down the heat a bit.

When the onion is translucent with a little browning, turn down the heat to medium-low (or low), add back in the steamed beans, the bacon, and the summer savory. Pour in the optional broth, or ¼ C water. If it all steams away instantly, add a little more liquid until a small puddle remains on the bottom of the pan. Stir everything together.

Clap the lid on and let it cook for another 5 minutes. Test for salt and pepper. Serve tasty and hot!

VARIATIONS.   Try this with any color of fresh summer bean (yellow, waxy, rattlesnake, speckled etc.). Try this with canned beans. Make up the bacon, onions, and herbs the same way, and then just heat the canned beans with the other ingredients at the end. This will work fine with the standard 14-ounce can.

Try other herbs with or instead of summer savory. Try combinations of herbs. It is really, really hard to go wrong adding fresh herbs to fresh produce. So just use what you can get your hands on. Delicate herbs like basil and cilantro can be stirred in just before serving.

Try adding spears of cut carrot about the same size as the beans. Or in a bean shortage make this with all carrots. Try other vegetables with or in place of the beans. Broccoli, cauliflower, kohlrabi, bokchoy, or even huge leaves of kale sliced up.

Try this with a sausage you find at your farmers market in place of the bacon. Try adding leftovers from this recipe to a salad.

If you have fresh shelling Old World beans like favas, edamame, or chick peas, remove the pods and thin skins, and cook them the same way as the pod beans. The cook time may be different so keep testing to determine when cooking is done for the beans you have.

MINTY PEAS WITH BUTTER ⌒

As a kid I hated peas — the squashy starchy things from the freezer case. But for a magical time each year I would get fresh peas. Those I loved. Fresh peas, picked, shelled and cooked all in the same day are crisp and sweet and worth all the trouble each and every year. Peas with mint was, and is, my very favorite way to eat them.

PREP TOGETHER.   Dump all the peas into a pile or in a large bowl. Begin to master the ancient art of shelling peas. Break off the stem end (it has the spiky or leafy cap) and remove the string by pulling it towards the other end of the pod. Use your thumb to tumble the peas into the clean bowl.

Toss the shell, stem and string into the "trash bowl." This is a skill that takes MANY pea pods to master. Don't despair. Your patience will be rewarded. Sample a few "raw runaway" peas, just to get a sense of what they taste like at the start. Pinch the mint leaves off their stems. Discard the stems, tear up the leaves and set aside.

COOK!   Fill a saucepan about 3/4 full of water, and bring to a boil. (Do not add salt; it will toughen the peas.) Carefully dump the cleaned peas into the water, and put on the lid. Wait 30 seconds after the water returns to the boil (I'm not kidding), and drain the peas. Put them in a serving bowl. Place the butter and mint in the bowl, and toss to coat the peas. Taste for salt; gingerly add a little and taste again until it is just right. Serve!

SERVES 2 – 4

1 LB PEAS IN SHELLS

SPRIGS OF MINT

1 TBS BUTTER

SALT

2 LARGE BOWLS (OR 3)

SAUCE PAN & LID

COLANDER

GRILLED FAVA BEANS

GRILL 4 – 6 PODS PER PERSON

FAVA BEANS

OIL

SALT

MEDIUM BOWL

SAUTÉ PAN OR GRILL

KITCHEN TOWEL

Make this when you are ready to find out what the big deal is with these big fuzzy legumes. Shelling and peeling the individual beans is a bit labor intensive, but the quick grilling recipe shares out the work and lets you see quickly why people continue to take the trouble.

PREP TOGETHER.   Separate the fava bean pods from their stems. Rinse them, and pat them dry. Place them in the bowl and toss with just enough oil to lightly coat the pods.

COOK!   Heat up a sauté pan or grill to medium-high heat. Place the fava bean pods in 1 layer on the hot surface (cook them in batches if you have lots). Let them cook for 4 to 6 minutes or until they start to blacken and soften. Turn them over, and cook the other side.

When the pods have black marks and have softened, set them aside to let them cool enough to handle. When you can pick them up, distribute a few to all diners. Have everyone open the pods, take out the beans, and pop the light green morsels out of the greenish-white skin. Sprinkle your little stack of treasures with a minute amount of salt and indulge in the deliciousness that has kept this fussy specimen on menus for centuries despite all the trouble.

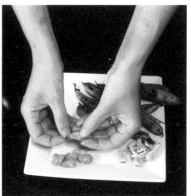

FAVA BEANS IN GARLICKY DRESSING ❧

This versatile recipe can be a mouth-watering appetizer, a wonderful salad addition, or delicious on a small piece of toast. The dressing brings out the sweetness of fresh shelling beans, and makes the most of summer garlic and herbs. Chilled, this makes excellent picnic food as well.

PREP TOGETHER. Open up the Fava bean pods, and remove the beans. Set them aside until you've boiled a pot of water (don't worry about the little green skins yet). Smash and peel the garlic, and chop it finely. Pick the parsley leaves off the large main stem, and chop them as well.

Make the dressing. In the serving bowl add the mayonnaise, vinegar, mustard, garlic, and parsley. Taste for seasoning, and add a little salt and pepper if it needs it. Whisk together the ingredients, and then slowly add the oil. (Or place all the dressing ingredients in a small snap-top container and give them a thorough shake. Taste for seasoning, and adjust the salt or pepper if it needs it.

COOK! Fill the soup pot ½ full with water, and set it on the stove on high heat to boil. Cover with the lid. When the water boils, drop all the fava beans in and boil them for 6 to 8 minutes or until the beans turn tender. To test, take one out, cut open the green skin and see if it has lost its raw firmness. Don't boil them over 10 minutes, or they may start to go mushy.

While the beans are boiling, add water to the ice in the large bowl to make an ice bath. When the beans are done, drain them in the colander, dump them in the icy water for a minute, then drain them in the colander again.

The beans should be cooked, and the pesky green skins will just pop off. Drop the peeled beans in the dressing, and let them sit for a minute or up to overnight. Enjoy the garlicky delights. If there are any leftovers, they'll be good for a few days longer.

VARIATIONS. As more heirloom varieties of Old World or shelling beans make their debut in farmers markets, this recipe will come in handy. Try smashing some of these beans with a fork, and spreading them on little toasts.

Try different herbs in the dressing, either alone or in combination. Summer savory gets along famously with beans. Add it in if you find some. Try stirring some fresh-chopped tomatoes in with the beans and dressing.

Try this with canned beans when you are craving fresh herb flavors or a lunch packed with protein. This is faster with the precooked beans, and there is no reason not to make the best food you can with the time you have and the supplies on hand.

QUICKEST SWEET CORN ♻

BOIL 1 – 2 EARS PER PERSON

1 – 2 EARS PER PERSON
....
WATER
....
SALT & BUTTER (OPTIONAL)
....

SOUP POT & LID
....
BAG FOR THE CORNHUSKS
....

SUBSTITUTIONS...
....
Or microwave cobs with the husk on.
1 ear = 2.5 minutes
2 ears = 5 minutes
4 ears = 9 minutes

When the first local corn of summer shows up, make this. And make it again later when you need a vegetable for dinner but don't have time to make anything. And then, make it again because it tastes so good. It is possibly the simplest vegetable to prepare, and while it lasts, it makes so many people happy.

PREP TOGETHER: Husk the corn. Grab the corn silk at the top, and some of the green husk, and pull down. Tear off all the green leaves and discard. Use a hand to brush and pull off the corn silk (a little left on the corn won't matter). Break off the stem that held the cornhusks, or leave it on as a handle. Do this anytime in the day before you plan to cook the corn. Wrap the cleaned corn in a kitchen towel and set aside until it is time to cook.

COOK! Fill a large pot $2/3$ full of water. Place it over high heat. Cover it! (Cook in batches if there is lots of corn.) When the water comes to a boil, place the corn in the water for no more than 4 minutes. Eat the corn as soon as it is cool enough to gingerly pick up. Try a bite! Roll it through the butter, and sprinkle on a little salt if you like.

VARIATIONS. Try these kernels the next day in a salad. Freeze them in a zip-top bag, and be sure to squeeze out the air. Try them mixed into cornbread. Try mixing them in salsa. Try adding them to a quesadilla.

Have leftover corn? Stand the cob on end on a cutting board. Use a knife to cut the kernels off by running it down the sides of the cob. No need to cut too deep.

GRILLED CORN ON THE COB

W hile getting the rest of the food ready to go, throw (OK, gently place) a few cobs on the grill for a spectacular summer cookout.

PREP TOGETHER. Bend back the cornhusks, and reach inside and pull out the corn silk. Cover the corn back up with the husks. If you would like to, and have time, soak the corn (husks on) in cold water for 10 minutes or longer. Do this anytime on the day the corn is going to be grilled. The cleaned corn can be wrapped in a barely damp kitchen towel and set aside until cooking time.

COOK! Heat the grill to medium. Place the corn in their husks on the grill, and cover. Give the corn a quarter turn every 8 minutes or so. Grill for about 25 minutes or until the kernels are tender. The husks will char, but that is part of what makes the corn taste so darn good. The corn can also be placed in a 400° F oven (no need to turn the corn). But it might take a bit longer.

VARIATIONS. Don't have so much time? Pull the husks off, and place the cobs directly on the grill. They'll cook in about half the time, and have a different flavor.

Try making a compound butter with the flavors of the rest of your food to spread on the cooked corn. Compound butters are made by letting butter soften by leaving it covered at room temperature for a few hours — or even overnight. Then the same flavors or spices from rubs, marinades, or sauces can be easily stirred in.

Note: in the interest of preventing contamination and upset tummies, never EVER stir in marinade that has been in contact with uncooked meats.

Try mixing in well chopped jalapeños and cilantro with some lemon or lime juice to go with South or Central American flavors. Try stirring in barbecue spices or a dry rub to pair with barbecued meats. Try mixing in the same herbs used on accompanying grilled meats.

GRILL 1 – 2 EARS PER PERSON

1 – 2 EARS PER PERSON

SALT

BUTTER

GRILL OR OVEN

LARGE SOAKING BOWL (OPTIONAL)

ROASTED PUMPKIN SEEDS

1 PUMPKIN = ABOUT 1.5 C SEEDS

SEEDS

SALT

OIL

VERY LARGE BOWL/PLUGGED SINK

COLANDER

BAKING SHEET

STIRRING SPATULA

KITCHEN TOWEL

I carve several Jack-O-Lanterns each year, just to get enough pumpkin seeds to last more than one day. This recipe actually works with a large variety of hard winter squash with thin-shelled seeds. In my experience, thin-shelled means I can easily bite a raw seed in half, without shaking my head or making any impolite noises.

PREP TOGETHER.   Take the membranous mess from the center of a pumpkin or squash, and put it in a sink or large bowl, full of water. Squeeze the seeds at their pointy end to pop them off the orange strings. The seeds will float on the surface.

Periodically scoop the loose seeds into the colander (over a towel). It is okay if there is still a little bit of orange string on the seeds; they don't need to be spotless. (Shooting seeds at each other, or at designated targets during the process, is entirely optional.)

COOK!   Heat the oven to 425°F. Rinse out the large bowl, dry it, and return the seeds to it. Toss the seeds with enough oil to coat them. Transfer the seeds to the baking sheet, and spread them out into approximately a single layer. Cook the seeds in batches, on two pans, rather than crowding. Bake for 15 minutes, remove the seeds from the oven, and lower the heat to 350°F.

Sprinkle with some salt and stir the seeds with the spatula to coat. Return the seeds to the oven for another 15 minutes or until they are light golden brown and temptingly crispy. Store any that aren't eaten immediately in an airtight container.

VARIATIONS.   Instead of plain salt, try barbecue rubs, Italian seasoning, and maybe some crushed red pepper. Leave out the salt and use a salt-free spice mixture, like curry powder.

Note: If you leave the seeds in the water for several hours (like I did once when I got distracted) and then roast them, the shells will pop in the oven. The extra water they soaked up turns into steam while trapped inside the shell, causing them to explode like popcorn in your oven. It sounds alarming, but it is a special treat.

roots

SWEET, PUNGENT, & STARCHY

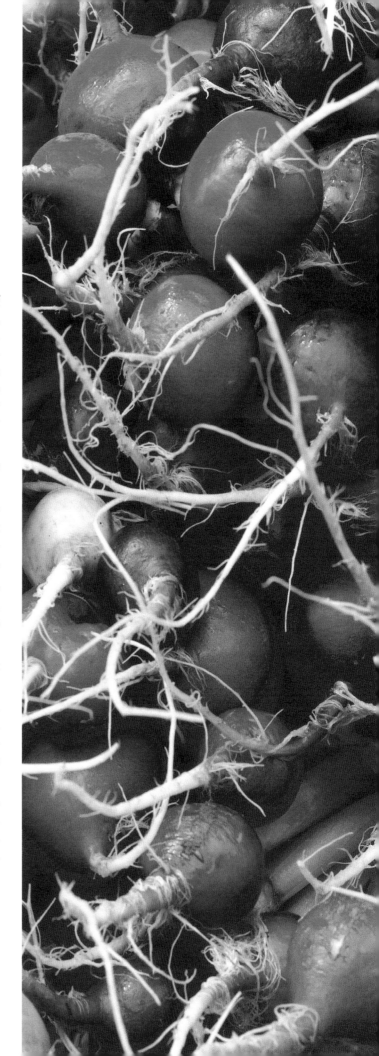

Does it grow underground? Is the rest of the plant growing out of it? Then it is a root. These usually show up near the end of the growing season (fennel is a definite exception), and can continue on when other crops are done, since they get to hang out protected from the cold in a cozy soil blanket. This means they may also show up first thing in the spring since they store so well.

Root vegetables can be roughly grouped into three categories:

Sweet. Salad stuff, things that could conceivably be eaten raw, are often roasted, and sometimes get added to baked goods. Examples are carrots, fennel (anise), parsnips, beets, jicama, and sunchokes.

Pungent. These roots all have distinctive, sometimes overpowering, flavors and are mostly eaten cooked. Examples are turnips, radishes, rutabagas or swedes, onions, shallots, and garlic.

Starchy. These are potatoes, yams, and things that act like potatoes.

As usual there are fence jumpers in this bunch too. Baby white turnips are sweet and tasty raw, and parsnip purée or boiled turnip has been known to step in for potatoes. But I don't know of anyone who likes a raw potato.

All roots have a particularly tasty side that can be brought out by baking, roasting, or frying them. This drives out excess water, toasts the sugars, and breaks down the starches. Try new things and find new favorites.

ONIONS, GARLIC AND SHALLOTS

PURCHASING. Look for dry papery skins with no sign of black spots or dark powder between the layers. They should by very firm and feel heavy for their size.

Exception: During the summer, fresh onions and shallots that haven't been dried for storage should be smooth and free of squishy spots.

STORAGE. If you have a cool dry spot, hang them in the net bags. If you have lots, check them occasionally so one bad onion doesn't ruin it for everybody. A counter top out of the sun will work for onions you'll use up in the next 2 to 3 weeks. They can also go in the fridge, but don't bag them up with the potatoes. They exchange chemicals that rot each other.

Garlic is happiest in a dark (non-refrigerated) box or drawer with reasonable circulation.

Fresh onions will be fine in the fridge, covered up for a few days, as are cut ones.

POTATOES

PURCHASING. Choose potatoes that are solid and have no squishy spots. Blemishes here and there are fine, especially little dry scars (living underground is tough). Potatoes that are suspiciously light often have a hollow center due to bugs of one sort or another. Dirty potatoes are not defective, they just need a good bath. As long as that dirt isn't covering up any squishy spots, it is just proof they were grown like the rest of potatoes, underground. Don't buy ones with green edges or ends (bitter!), and don't buy ones with roots or shoots growing out of the eyes (stored too long or wrong).

STORAGE. Potatoes are fine on a counter for several days. Or they can be kept in a dark, cool, dry place for a nice long time in a net or breathable cloth or paper bag. Keep them in the fridge in a paper bag away from the onions, and they will be good until you get around to them — though they are produce and won't actually last forever. If your potatoes start to spout, cut off those bits, and cook them in something right away.

TURNIPS, BEETS, RADISHES, CARROTS, FENNEL OR ANISE, PARSNIPS AND SO ON

PURCHASING. Again, go for firm and heavy. Stay away from limp. If the greens on top look like they would be good to eat, bonus! It is the sign of ultimate freshness and extra tasty food. Buy the root, and cut off the green tops right away so the root stops feeding the greens, and will feed you instead. See the Leaves chapter for what to do with the greens.

Carrots are the most fragile of this hearty group. They are a whole different vegetable when truly fresh and are especially fine when enjoyed raw. Large specimens store well and are pleasing when cooked. They are a member of the parsley family, and the greens are edible if you want to try them.

Fennel bulbs should be heavy and firm with tightly bunched layers. The feathery fronds can be chopped as an herb or used to stuff poultry or fish when it is roasted or grilled. The woody shoots can be added to charcoal to produce fragrant smoke for grilling or added to stock for extra flavor.

The rest of the roots are fine new or old, but some will get more pungent with age. Make sure the stem end doesn't look black and slimy or have large dry cracks. Both are signs of poor storage. In all cases, a little mud or dirt is not a blemish, just proof of being grown in the dirt.

STORAGE. Any "baby" versions should be eaten up soon. They are full of fragile, tasty flavors and should be enjoyed. They will keep for a day on the counter, and a few more in the fridge.

Full grown versions, well, we named the root cellar after them in honor of their storability. Keep them cool and keep them from getting too wet or too dry. Bagged in a fridge or on their own in the "crisper" drawer will keep small amounts in great shape for a nice long time.

Check the Bibliography (see page 150) for other places to find information on larger scale storage.

HERB ROASTED POTATOES

SERVES 2 – 4

1 LB POTATOES

2 TSP OIL

A FEW SPRIGS OF ROSEMARY

SALT & PEPPER

KITCHEN TOWELS

SCRUBBY BRUSH

BAKING SHEET

MEASURING SPOONS

SHARP KNIFE (KID KNIFE–OPTIONAL)

CUTTING BOARD

Roasted potatoes are a great recipe to start while sorting out the rest of a meal. The fluffy, slightly crispy potatoes are excellent for breakfast, lunch, or dinner. Even better, it adjusts effortlessly to your needs, supplies, and tastes. And if that wasn't enough, re-heated leftovers are just as tasty the next day.

PREP TOGETHER.   Wash the potatoes well in a sink or a large bowl of water. Scrub vigorously with a scrubby brush to remove any dust or mud. If they are particularly dirty, a second wash may be necessary. Sort the potatoes. Teeny tiny potatoes can be left whole and stabbed once or twice with a fork. Larger potatoes should be cut into large bite size pieces. Strip the needles off the rosemary sprigs. Keep the needles and discard the stems.

COOK!   Heat the oven to 425°F. Place all the potatoes on the baking sheet, and pour on the oil. Sprinkle the potatoes with about 1 tsp of salt, about ½ tsp of pepper, and all the herbs. Use clean hands to mix the potatoes and everything else.

Spread the potatoes out in the baking sheet. Roast in the oven for about 25 to 30 min. Watch the potatoes. If they begin to get a little brown at the edges, they are probably ready. When they are fork tender, they are done. No raw potato crunch should be left. Let them cool a bit and serve!

VARIATIONS.   Try adding what herbs you have available. Add a mix of herbs such as parsley, basil, oregano, dill, and maybe a little mint. Try adding grated or crumbled cheese to the hot potatoes when you take them out of the oven.

Try with sweet potatoes if they are available. Try with spice mixtures instead of herbs such as season salt, paprika, oregano, and curry. If there are leftovers, chop them smaller (large pea sized), sauté them with onions to make a hash that goes great with eggs and perks up all sorts of leftovers. Try leftover potatoes warmed up, and stirred with a little vinaigrette dressing for a very French potato salad. Throw in a little cooked bacon or sausage, and you can feel very Swiss.

RAW BABY BEET SALAD

Beets can be daunting enough, but really, raw beets? Don't worry, this only works with little tiny, non-threatening, baby beets. And if you can get a hold of Chioggia, candy-stripe or candy-cane beets, or golden beets, all the better. No matter what kind of tiny beet you get, this makes a surprising, and nonthreatening, way to try beets for the very first time.

PREP TOGETHER.   Cut the roots and leaves off the beets. Use the vegetable peeler to peel the thin skin off the beets. Using the knife or vegetable peeler (or mandoline) make the thinnest slices possible of raw beets.

COOK!   Toss with the oil, vinegar, salt, and pepper. Start with a teaspoon of oil and vinegar, and add sparingly from there. Taste and adjust until it comes out just right.

VARIATIONS.   Try eating this with bleu cheese on crackers, if you are feeling daring.

SERVES 2 – 4

2 – 4 BABY BEETS

TASTY OLIVE OIL

MILD VINEGAR

SALT & PEPPER

SCRUBBY BRUSH

KITCHEN TOWELS

CUTTING BOARD

SHARP KNIFE

VEGETABLE PEELER
(MANDOLINE - OPTIONAL)

SALAD BOWL AND SERVERS

ROASTED BEETS
WITH OIL & VINEGAR DRESSING ✎

SERVES 2 – 4

1 LB BEETS

2 TBS TASTY OLIVE OIL

1 TBS VINEGAR (CIDER OR BALSAMIC)

1 TSP DIJON STYLE MUSTARD

SALT & PEPPER

1 – 2 GARLIC CLOVES (OPTIONAL)

SCRUBBY BRUSH

CUTTING BOARD

SHARP KNIFE

PARING KNIFE/SERRATED BUTTER KNIFE

SMALL BOWL

MEASURING SPOONS

FORK/WHISK

BAKING PAN

SALAD BOWL & SERVERS

Make this when faced with your first big, red beets. No getting around it, beets have a sweet, earthy flavor. Some people find the sweetness odd, and others contend that "earthy" is a way of saying "tastes like dirt." There's some truth to that, but with the right amount of vinegar (and garlic) the earthiness is transformed, and the complex, tasty flavors shine through.

PREP TOGETHER. Use the sharp knife to cut the leaves and fuzzy roots off the beets. Use a scrubby brush to thoroughly clean the beets in plenty of water. Rinse well. If they need it, give the beets one more scrub and rinse. Beets get just as dirty as potatoes.

Place them in the baking pan. (No oil, no foil, no nothing.) Baby beets can stay whole. Consider cutting larger beets in halves or quarters. Otherwise they may take an hour or more to cook.

Mix together the vinegar, mustard, salt, and pepper in a small bowl (smash, peel, and finely chop the optional garlic). Stir together with the fork or whisk. Slowly add in the oil while stirring. The amounts of dressing ingredients are starting points. Adjust them to your taste. (All the dressing ingredients can also be placed in a small tightly lidded container and shaken.)

If the beet leaves are very fresh, nibble on the washed greens like bunnies do. Dip them in the vinaigrette to test it. (Baby beet greens are so tender they can even be used raw in salad.)

Once you are happy with the dressing, set it aside. Give it a good stir or shake right before it gets used.

Note: Beets and chard are such close relatives they are actually the same species (*Beta vulgaris*). Taste a chard stem with beets in mind, and you'll see what I mean. This means you can, and should, cook fresh beet greens the same way you would cook chard and other hearty greens.

COOK! Heat the oven to 375°F. Place the pan of cleaned beets in the oven for about 20 to 35 minutes. Beets of different size, shape, and age will take different times to cook. Beets are done when a knife enters them easily (they are "knife tender").

Remove the cooked beets from the oven, and let them cool until they can be handled. Peel them by pulling the skin off. Use a paring knife (or serrated butter knife) to help remove stubborn spots. Wash your hands right away if you want to avoid the dreaded "pink-finger."

Cut beets into quarters, half-moons, very thin slices, or small cubes, and toss with the dressing. Eat warm, or cool. Delicious with garlic bread.

VARIATIONS. Try adding a flavorful cheese to this salad for added punch and balancing the sharp cheese with sweet, roasted nuts. Try adding baby or chopped bitter greens to balance the sweetness of the beets. Try squeezing lime or lemon juice over the salad — or in place of the vinegar in the dressing.

SUBSTITUTIONS...

Cheese:
bleu cheese
goat cheese
feta

Nuts:
pecans
hazelnuts
almonds
pistachios

Greens:
risée
radicchio
endive
baby kale

Citrus:
orange or grapefruit slices
a squeeze of lemon or lime

WARM FENNEL & PURPLE CABBAGE SLAW ❧

This slaw is the opposite of coleslaw, savory and a bit salty rather than the usual sweet and sour balance. Make this when you need a hearty vegetable to stand up and support a meaty main dish. Or when you find yourself facing fennel and cabbage. I love it with pork (BBQ, grilled, pan roasted, and so on). Raw fennel is tough, but the sweat at the start of the recipe makes it sweet and crunchy. Black bean sauce is the secret ingredient.

PREP TOGETHER. Cut the cabbage and fennel into quarters, through the stem. Slice out the tough solid core piece from both vegetables. Cut the onion in half, and peel off the dry outer layers. Then thinly slice the onion, cabbage, and fennel.

In the bottom of the salad bowl, with a fork or whisk, briskly stir the black bean sauce, rice vinegar, salt, and pepper. Continue to stir, and slowly add in the oil. (All dressing ingredients can be placed in a tightly sealing container and shaken.) Toss with ½ of the sliced onion, and set aside.

COOK! Heat a sauté pan over medium-low heat with the 2 tsp oil for 3 to 4 minutes. Stir in the fennel and ½ tsp salt, and begin to sweat and soften the fennel. This will take several minutes, so keep stirring it every few minutes and checking for softening. If the fennel begins to brown, turn down the heat. You want something that still has a little crunch and plenty of body.

If after 8 minutes or so, the fennel is still tough, add the water, turn up the heat to medium-high, and let the fennel simmer.

As the fennel approaches done, add the rest of the sliced sweet onion, and continue to stir to soften.

When the fennel and onion are just about done, add in the cabbage, and stir to combine. Let this sit over medium heat for about 5 minutes to warm and just soften the cabbage.

Add the warm vegetables straight from the stovetop to the dressing and onion mixture. Stir to combine. Taste, and add any extra vinegar, salt or pepper until it is just right.

Chinese black bean sauce often also comes with garlic. Either variation works fine. It keeps nearly forever in your refrigerator. It is one of those pungent condiments that is overpowering when tasted alone. But used as a background flavor, it has "secret ingredient" power.

It is usually available in the "Ethnic" or "Asian" section of large grocery stores.

VARIATIONS. Try a regular onion, if that's what is on hand. But only add 1/8 to ¼ of the onion raw to the dressing. Soften most of the onion with the fennel.

Try grating some other vegetables in with the sliced cabbage, like carrots, parsnips, or radishes. Try this with Korean Short Ribs (Bulgogi) or other salty grilled meats.

FENNEL, BEET, & GOAT CHEESE SALAD

SERVES 3 – 6

3 – 4 BABY BEETS

1 SMALL FENNEL BULB

1 BABY ONION

3 TBS GOAT CHEESE

OIL

DRESSING:

1 TBS VINEGAR

JUICE FROM ½ AN ORANGE

1 SMALL HANDFUL FEATHERY PARTS OF THE FENNEL STEMS

1 TSP GOAT CHEESE

1 GARLIC CLOVE

SALT & PEPPER TO TASTE

1 TBS TASTY OLIVE OIL

SCRUBBY BRUSH

BAKING PAN

SHARP KNIFE

CUTTING BOARD

SAUTÉ PAN

STIRRING SPATULA

FORK/WHISK

SALAD BOWL AND SERVERS

Each ingredient has strong flavors. Fennel is crunchy, with a slight licorice flavor, beets are uniquely savory-sweet, and the goat cheese is creamy with a pleasant tanginess. This salad is a balancing act that highlights the best of each ingredient. Make this salad as a special treat for yourself, or as a surprising part of a meal for people you really like.

PREP TOGETHER. Heat the oven to 450°F. Trim the leaves and the fuzzy root end off the beets. Give them a good scrub, and rub some oil on them. (Cut large beets in half first.) Place them in a single layer in the smallest pan they'll fit in. Place them in the oven for 40 to 50 minutes. They are done when a knife slides in easily.

Let the beets cool, and scrub or peel the skins off. Wash your hands immediately to avoid the dreaded "pink finger." Chop roughly into large bite-size pieces.

Cut the onion in half through the root, and peel off the dry layers. Slice the onion thinly. Cut the green stalks off the top of the fennel bulb. Chop up a small handful of the light feathery fronds and set them aside. Cut the fennel bulb in half, removing any tough outer layers. Cut the tough core out of the center. Slice the fennel as thin as possible.

To make the dressing, smash, peel and chop the garlic. Stir together the juice or vinegar, goat cheese, garlic, fennel fronds, salt, and pepper. Slowly add the tasty oil while stirring the dressing with a fork or whisk. (All dressing ingredients can be placed in a small snap-top container and shaken.)

COOK! Place a sauté pan with a little regular oil over medium heat. After 2 to 3 minutes, add the fennel and onion with a sprinkle of salt. These need to sweat or heat up over gentle heat to soften and release moisture. There should be little or no sizzling. Take them off the heat when they have lost that raw "squeakiness," but are still crisp.

Combine all the fennel and onions with the beet pieces, and pour the dressing over them. Stir only a few times to avoid turning everything pink. Scatter the rest of the crumbled goat cheese over the salad. A couple of pieces of bread, brushed with olive oil, and toasted make great croûtons.

VARIATIONS.   Try making this in the spring with green garlic or garlic chutes or scapes in place of the garlic.

Try green onions if no bulb onions are available. Try adding early or baby lettuce leaves to this salad. Try adding citrus fruit segments like orange, tangerine, or grapefruit. Try with bleu cheese in place of goat cheese. Try adding some nuts to this salad as well.

SUBSTITUTIONS...

No tiny cabbages? ¼ of a regular sized one
No baby beets? 2 fist sized beets
Only regular sized onions? Use about ¼ .
No orange? Use 2Tbs balsamic vinegar

Cheese:
Cream cheese or other soft cheeses
Thick plain yogurt
Sharp flavored creamy cheeses

Produce:
green onions
garlic scapes
early lettuces

ROASTED ROOT VEGETABLES ↩

Choose a mix of potatoes, beets, parsnips, onions, and carrots or some other set of starchy, sweet, and earthy roots. Bake them until they are lightly browned and slightly shriveled. This means the flavors have been concentrated, and the sugars caramelized, which changes the vegetables from an obligation to delicious. And the news gets even better. Once baked, root vegetables freeze for months making them a quick addition to any dinner.

PREP TOGETHER. Scrub and rinse any muddy or dusty root vegetables. Cut off the stems, fuzzy roots, and other inedible bits. Peel off tough outer skins with the vegetable peeler.

Cut the onion in half through the root end and peel off the dry outer layers. Cut up all the vegetables into largish bite-size pieces. If beets are tougher, make them thinner. The onions are tender, so those pieces can be a bit larger. Chop up the sage (and other herbs) into little pieces.

COOK! Heat the oven to 425°F. Place all the prepared vegetables on the baking sheet. Sprinkle with the oil and 1 tsp of salt. Toss with clean hands to coat all the vegetables. Bake for 20 minutes.

Remove the vegetables from the oven, and turn the heat down to 375°F. Stir the 1 Tbs balsamic vinegar and the sage (and any extra herbs) into the vegetables with another pinch of salt and a sprinkle of pepper.

Return the vegetables to the oven. Bake for 15 to 25 minutes or until the vegetables (especially the beets) are fork tender. The pale vegetables should start to get brown edges, and all the vegetables should look a bit shriveled.

When they are finished, transfer the vegetables to a bowl. Taste for vinegar, salt, and pepper. Sprinkle, stir, taste, and repeat until delicious.

This is a perfect make lots once, freeze part for later, dish. Once the roots have baked the first 20 minutes a little freeze and thaw won't hurt them. Freeze what you want to use later in zip-top bags or other freezer safe containers in the portion sizes you'll want.

To use from frozen: Heat the oven to 375°F. Spread the vegetables out on a baking sheet or pan. Toss with the Tbs of vinegar, and add sage or other herbs and a sprinkle of salt and pepper. Roast for at least 25 minutes.

Again, check for tenderness, browning, and intensified flavor.

VARIATIONS. Try adding hearty leafy greens along with the root vegetables. Clean and tear up some hearty leafy greens into hand-sized pieces. Try kale, chard, collards, mustard, beet, or turnips greens. Chard, beet, and turnip stems are edible, but the rest must be stripped off their tough, woody stems. Add them in with the vegetables at the beginning.

Try adding greens and bacon. Heat 1 slice of bacon, chopped into small pieces, in a sauté pan until crispy. Remove the bacon (save for the end), but leave the rendered fat. Toss in some hearty leafy greens, stir to coat them, and sauté until they start to look a bit wilted. Add them into the vegetables when baking them the rest of the way at 375°F. Sprinkle the bacon over the vegetables as you serve them.

Try sprinkling some truffle salt over the vegetables just before serving for an extra fancy, super-savory touch. Add other herbs if you have some on hand.

SUBSTITUTIONS...

Try for a mix of starchy, sweet & earthy:
potatoes (starchy)
sweet potatoes (sweet)
beets (earthy)
parsnips (earthy)
onions (sweet)
carrots (sweet)
turnips (earthy)

TASTY TURNIPS (TRUST ME!) ♋

SERVES 4 – 6

6 – 8 BABY OR 2 – 3 LARGE TURNIPS

GREENS FROM VERY FRESH TURNIPS
(OPTIONAL)

½ AN ONION

1 C WATER

SALT & PEPPER

1 TBS VINEGAR

OIL

SCRUBBY BRUSH

SHARP KNIFE

VEGETABLE PEELER

CUTTING BOARD

MEDIUM POT & LID

MEASURING CUP & SPOONS

FORK

When turnips turn up in the veggie box (that joke never gets old), this is what to do with them. Stovetop turnips and greens are a Southern tradition. Done wrong, with too much water for too long, produces khaki mush with flavorless white blobs. Done right, you create a kitchen sensation that can go on to surprising other lives.

PREP TOGETHER. Scrub the turnips clean, cut off the leaves and fuzzy roots. If the leaves are fresh, keep them and clean them as well. If they are tough, turning yellow, or just look unappetizing, go ahead and discard them.

Peel the turnips and cut into cubes about the size of the top joint of your thumb. Cut the onion in half through the root, and peel off the dry outer layers. Lay the onion down on the flat side. Make three cuts toward the root end, but not all the way through it. This should divide the onion half approximately into quarters. Cut the onion into thick slices.

If using the greens, cut or tear the washed leaved into pieces a little smaller than the palm of your hand.

COOK! Place the medium pot over medium-high heat with about 2 tsp oil in the bottom. Heat for 3 minutes or until a small piece of onion in the pot begins to sizzle. Then add the rest of the onion and a pinch of salt. Stir the onion until it is very noisy, smells oniony, and is well coated with the oil.

Add the cubed turnip (and optional greens). Stir over medium-high heat for a minute or two. Pour in the 1 C water or broth, lower the heat to medium, and cover for about 15 minutes. The temperature should still be high enough that steam is escaping occasionally, but the pot should not be boiling vigorously.

After 15 minutes, use a fork to test the turnips. Cook until the turnips are fork tender. When this happens, remove the lid and keep cooking until most of the liquid is gone. Remove from the heat. Stir in the vinegar and any herbs. Taste and adjust the salt and pepper to your taste.

VARIATIONS.   Try adding some thinly sliced bacon or ham when sautéing the onions. Add more savory flavor by using broth instead of water.

Try adding a half-pound of potatoes. Cook them with the turnips the same way, but continue the cooking until the turnips and potatoes are very soft. Mash together the potatoes, turnips, and other ingredients. Add enough milk or cream or butter or broth to make tasty mashed turnips.

Try thinning out the mashed turnip and potato variation from above with even more broth. Now it's a soup. Top with a little crispy bacon and fried sage leaves.

SUBSTITUTIONS...

rutabaga

swede

THE RADISH PROBLEM ❧

MAKE 2 – 4 RADISHES PER PERSON

SOLUTION #1 INGREDIENTS:

4 – 6 RADISHES

1 TBS VINEGAR

2 TBS WATER

1 TBS SUGAR

½ TSP SALT

SCRUBBY BRUSH

CUTTING BOARD

KNIFE

SAUCEPAN

MEASURING CUPS

MEASURING SPOONS

SPOON

SMALL BOWL

SNAP TOP CONTAINER

Why are radishes a problem? Radishes grow first, grow easily, and are so pretty. Little kids are excited and tempted by the attractive radish, until they bite into their first one. I didn't give up, and neither should you. Fight back and make the radish great. The pungent spicy bite of the radish can be tricky to work with, but it has at least three simple solutions. I have been searching for the radish solution since I was faced with the related "kid plus dirt" problem. This is all you need for three tasty radish bites; sour, buttery, and complicated sweet.

SOLUTION #1   The fastest. This is a garnish for meat, salads, and munching plain or with sharp cheese. Slice off the roots and leaves. Scrub them clean. Cut the radishes in half and slice as thin as possible. Place the slices in a small bowl. Stir with the vinegar, water, sugar, and salt. Let it sit until slightly pink. Ready! Enjoy. (If the radishes have no red, then wait about 10 minutes.)

SOLUTION #2   This method is definitely French. It requires butter and works best with tiny or mild radishes, such as the infamous French Breakfast Radish. Keep the leaves on the radishes to use as handles. Cut off the roots, and scrub them super clean. To enjoy, hold a radish by the leaves, dip it in the melted butter, touch to a little salt, and eat it up.

SOLUTION #3.   This gives a very Japanese flavor: sweet, sour, salty, and pungent. It's better with large and very large radishes — watermelon and daikon are the best. Scrub the radishes. Trim off the leaves and fuzzy roots. Cut the radishes into medium-thin slices or wedges, and place in a snap-top container or jar with a lid. Pour the water, rice vinegar, salt, and sugar in the saucepan. Bring the mixture to a boil. Keep it there for 4 minutes, stirring to dissolve all the sugar and salt. Pour the hot liquid over the radishes. Cover, cool, and refrigerate overnight.

Opening the refrigerator the next morning, you will face the sulfurous nature of the radish. It will all be worth it to experience the crunchy, sour, mildly peppery, and sweet essence of the Japanese pickle.

Enjoy with anything meaty and/or salty.

SOLUTION #2 INGREDIENTS:

RADISHES (SMALL)
....

SALT
....

MELTED BUTTER
....

SOLUTION #3 INGREDIENTS:

RADISHES (DAIKON IS BEST)
....

1 C VINEGAR (RICE)
....

$^2/_3$ C WATER
....

$^2/_3$ C SUGAR
....

2 TBS SALT
....

resources

conventions & further reading

ingredients

equipment

produce identification guide

CONVENTIONS & FURTHER READING

ookbooks use abbreviations for measurements, techniques, and ingredients and all sorts of other information they use all the time. However, if you are just beginning, or working with a brand new cook, they can be mysterious and unhelpful. As you gain experience, these gain meaning. So, here is a small section on the conventions used in this cookbook. If "blanch," "tsp," and the meaning of "fork tender" are clear, skip this section. If such language creates confusion or frustration, read on.

Abbreviations, generalizations, and common techniques are briefly explained here so that recipes can be kept reasonably short. I am certain each and every one of these terms has a more technical and precise definition. This section is meant for quick reference to get you started. As you gain proficiency and have more specific questions, check out bigger, badder cookbooks. (Check the bibliography of this book, and as always, there is much more to be found online.)

MEASUREMENTS

tsp. teaspoon. 3 tsp = 1Tbs. Estimation = a small pile in your palm.

Tbs. tablespoon. 1 Tbs = 3 tsp, 2 Tbs = 1 fluid ounce (fl. oz.), 4 Tbs = ¼ C. Estimation = a shallow handful.

C. cup. 1 C = 8 fl. oz., 2 C = 1 pint, 4 C = 1 quart. Metric cooking is all in milliliters (ml) and grams (g). (No silly conversions)

PREPARATION

chop. Cut up the food into pieces of about the same size so they cook at the same speed. No need for regular shapes of any kind.

dice. I'm not talking perfect cubes here, but try for blocky pieces of close to similar size. When you go into the restaurant business, you can get out your ruler and protractor. Until then, relax.

grate or shred. Get out a grater. If you have a food processor of some sort lurking in your cupboard, this is where it can shine.

peel. Take off the outer part. Sometimes this is edible, but for the purposes of the recipe, it makes sense to remove it. Use a vegetable peeler if a knife feels clumsy.

slice. Flat pieces. Again, try for similar thicknesses. No need to get out a ruler; the measurements are just there to give an idea of thick or thin.

smash. I often place things under the flat of my knife and hit it with the heel of my hand. Or use the bottom of a pan, or one of those meat mallet things. All are satisfying and effective.

stir. Move things around in the pan or bowl to make sure they are mixed. There should be no large islands of one ingredient separate from the rest of the mixture. Do so gently or vigorously as the recipe suggests.

toss. Use a large bowl or pan, and move the ingredients up and around, bringing the pieces at the bottom to the top. This is used to make sure all of the something is coated with something else (salad with dressing, potatoes with oil, etc.).

whisk. Do this with a fork, or preferably, with a wire whisk. The goal is to rapidly stir things in a circular motion, and add air at the same time. Mixing together the white and the yolk of an egg so the whole thing is light yellow is a classic whisking task. Putting the same stuff in a leak-proof container and shaking hard can do the same thing.

COOKING

blanch. Briefly boiling an ingredient, then immersing it a bath of half-ice and half-water. This is often used with vegetables to remove bitter or stinky components, or to prepare them for freezing or preserving. Boiling times can range from seconds to 10 minutes, depending on your vegetable. Larger pieces and harder vegetable take longer, smaller and more tender vegetables will take less. See the following table for estimates of boiling time.

Vegetable Type	Example	Blanching Time
baby vegetables	baby turnips, baby zucchini	2 to 3 minutes
hearty leaves	kale, collards	3 minutes
tender leaves	spinach, chard	1.5 to 2 minutes
Brussels sprouts	whole	4 minutes
	halved	2 minutes
beets	baby	15 to 20 minutes
	larger – whole	35 minutes
turnips	halves	8 to 20 minutes
salad vegetables (something you might eat raw)	carrots – cut	2 to 4 minutes
	kohlrabi – cut	3 to 5 minutes
	green beans	3 minutes
	cauliflower	3 minutes
	broccoli	2 minutes
Mystery?	Cut into uniform pieces	Take out at knife tender

boil. Immersing ingredients in water that is rolling and bubbling (at 212°F or 100°C). A low boil means a few bubbles appear each second but the liquid in the pot is largely still. A rolling boil is when all the liquid is rolling around bubbling vigorously, and the bubbles are uncountable.

braise. Cooking covered for longer amounts of time, at lower temperatures in a little bit of liquid. This is used to make tough things tender and develop more complex flavors. A contrasting technique to sautéing or boiling.

caramelize. Gently burning the sugar in a food. All produce has some natural sugars, but fruits and some vegetables, like carrots and onions, are packed with them. When they are cooked until brown their flavors become sweeter and slightly toasty. In the modern kitchen, caramelize has become a catch-all replacement for "brown," literally cooking food so it turns brown (for example, brown the onions and ground beef) and no longer is strictly limited to sugar-containing foods.

fry. A layer of oil (¼ inch or deeper, depending) is heated to around 350°F for the purpose of cooking food. Fried foods are crispy since most of the water has been driven out, and the structure of starch molecules (usually) in the food has been altered. Extremely tasty.

fork tender. Literally, easily pierced with a fork. A way to test if the tough parts of a food have been broken down and softened by cooking. A variant of fork tender is knife tender, when the food is less tender than the fork test. Some foods have fibers that never completely soften, sometimes you want to stop the cooking sooner, and some foods get an unpleasant texture or taste if they get too soft, so they get the knife test instead of the fork test.

grill. Cooking anything on a rack close to a high heat source. Charcoal and gas grills are what we most often think of, but remember, an oven broiler is an upside down grill.

roast. Cooking something at a moderate heat inside a (mostly) closed box (usually an oven). Most people think of roasting meats, but vegetables can get the same treatment for new textures and flavors. (This is interchangeable in this book with the term "baking.")

sauté. Cooking in a flat pan with a little oil heated over medium-high to high heat. Small pieces of food are moved about rapidly for quick cooking. The root word is "jump" in French, for an idea of what you are trying to do.

simmer. Cooking a food in water at a temperature just below boiling. In this book it means steaming with only occasional bubbling, or bubbles at the edges.

sweat. Soften a food without browning. Onions and other firm aromatic vegetables (for example, celery, carrots, fennel) are cooked in a shallow pan over medium to medium-low heat with a little salt and oil. The vegetables will release their juices (sweat out liquid) and intensify flavors, but without any browning or caramelization. This is what recipes are asking you to do when they direct you to "cook the onions until translucent."

toast or broil. Inside grilling. Food on a rack with only one side exposed to the heat at a time. Think toasted cheese sandwich.

BIBLIOGRAPHY

Ready to go beyond the basics? Here are the best books I read to help me answer some of the questions I had when learning to cook, and writing this book. It seems like a short list for a lifetime of cooking. But much of my early source material included recipes off the back of the Libby's pumpkin can, off the sides of cereal boxes, my mom's cookie, casserole and breakfast recipes and scribbles about food I found tasty. The best thing I figured out early on is, food is forgiving, especially produce. If you start with guidance on cooking times and temperatures, then all that needs to be done is fuss with seasonings, keep tasting and ask for input.

COOKBOOKS

Brown, Alton. *I'm Just Here for the Food: Food + Heat = Cooking*. New York: Stewart, Tabori & Chang, 2002.
What's so great about this book? More food science than you can wave a pH meter at. Written for the science novice and very useful for learning to cook from basic concepts – or off book.

Child, Julia, Louisette Bertholle and Simone Beck. *Mastering the Art of French Cooking: Volume 1*. New York: Borzoi Books, 1961.
What's so great about this book? This is where I first learned the art of ingredient substitution. The master recipe format of this cookbook can be frustrating at first, but liberating in the end. Again, the real secret ingredient to amazing food is not magic, just time and practice.

Child, Julia. *Julia's Kitchen Wisdom*. New York: Borzoi Books, 2000.
What's so great about this book? If you are in a hurry, skip the big book, and look here for the highlights – pie dough, quiche, cake, crêpes, roast chicken. Most of us are never going to cook lamb kidneys anyway.

Cunningham, M. *Fannie Farmer Cookbook*. New York: Alfred A. Knopf,1990.

Farmer, F.M. *Boston Cooking School Cookbook*. Boston: Little Brown & Co., 1944.
What's so great about these books? They are the earlier half of the soul of early modern (stove rather than fireplace) American cooking. A simplified version of almost every dish of American food you've ever eaten is in one of these books.

Guste Jr., Roy F. *Antoine's Cookbook*. New York: W.W. Norton & Company, 1980.
What's so great about this book? This is the book that brought it home that excellent food lies in the choice of ingredients and the attention of the cook. There's no magic or secret piece of equipment.

Kafka, Barbara and Christopher Styler. *Vegetable Love*. New York: Artisan, 2005.
What's so great about this book? If it wasn't anywhere else, the vegetable would be here. But some of the recipes are down right odd.

Katzen, Mollie. *The Moosewood Cookbook: New Revised Edition*. Berkeley: Ten Speed Press, 1992.
What's so great about this book? My first glimpse into real cooking with vegetables. They are more than a side dish.

McGee, Harold. *On Food and Cooking: The Science and Lore of the Kitchen 2nd Ed*. New York: Scribner, 2004.
What's so great about this book? In one handy, well-organized volume, it holds much of the useful information and enjoyable trivia I spent a lifetime bumbling about and discovering. And then some more.

Oliver, Jamie. *Cook with Jamie: My Guide to Making you a Better Cook*. New York: Hyperion, 2007.
What's so great about this book? Six things: 1. Clear and simple buying instructions for red meat. 2. Butchering instructions and photos for fish and poultry. 4. Basic tutorials on making breads, pastas and simple desserts. 5. The combinations of fresh, simple to find ingredients into exotic flavors. 6. The informal, inviting tone.

Passmore, Jackie. *Lett's Companion to Asian Food and Cooking*. London: Letts of London, 1991.
What's so great about this book? This book helped me learn to navigate grocery stores where I cannot read most of the labels. It's also where I learned to make a Thai curry as rich and complex as anything I'd had at a restaurant.

Rather, Rebecca, and Alison Oresman. *The Pastry Queen: Royally Good Recipes from the Texas Hill Country's Rather Sweet Bakery & Café*. Berkeley: Ten Speed Press, 2004.
What's so great about this book? It is an excellent, modern baking book for the dabbler and amateur. Big flavors in baking categories that appeal to the modern cook.

Rombauer, Irma S., and Marion Rombauer Becker. *Joy of Cooking.* New York: Scribner, 2006. (Multiple editions, I have 1953.)

What's so great about this book? This book captures the more modern half of America's cooking spirit. If it's not in Fannie Farmer, it's here. My most treasured volume is from the 1950s and makes me happy to live in the age of food processors and soy sauce. Here, avocados are called "alligator pears."

Rosene, Marcella. *Pasta & Co. The Cookbook.* Seattle, WA: Pasta and Company, 1987.

What's so great about this book? Rich, flavorful food made with staple and easy to find ingredients. They have newer books that are easier to get which follow the same theme.

Seed, Diane. *Favorite Indian Food.* Berkeley: Ten Speed Press, 1990.

What's so great about this book? Indian food with training wheels. Just enough information to get started, but not so much to get intimidated and quit.

Segnit, Niki. *The Flavour Thesaurus.* London: Bloomsbury, 2010.

What's so great about this book? Inspiration for when I get in a rut, or when I am feeling particularly adventurous. Excellent for learning how to color outside the lines with your cooking.

Smith, Jeff. *The Frugal Gourmet.* New York: Ballantine Books, 1987.

What's so great about this book? Another book showing that starting with regular, but whole ingredients is the ticket to amazing food. The only secret is spending the time and learning the skills.

Sommerville, Annie. *Field of Greens.* New York: Bantam, 1993.

What's so great about this book? Introduced the idea of gourmet vegetables. (What? I know!) My eyes were opened wider to the possibilities of produce.

WEBSITES

Using websites is a great way to explore ideas or about food, or to hunt for a new way of doing something. These are my favorite for general knowledge, a sort of recipe wiki. Each has it's own style, and you'll find one you like best.

All Recipes. http://allrecipes.com/recipes/

Epicurious. http://www.epicurious.com

Food Network. "Food Network Recipes" http://www.foodnetwork.com/

PRESERVING INFORMATION

If you are looking to preserve more produce than a bag or two of frozen zucchini shreds, or a few containers of applesauce, look here. These are the people who know, have tested and tested, and eaten more pickles than I can shake a stick at.

Jarden Home Brands. *Ball Blue Book Guide to Preserving.* Daleville, IN: Heathmark LLC, 2011.

What's so great about this book? This is the bible of home canning and preserving. The instructions and recipes are simple and straightforward. Extensive information for canning and freezing. And it deals with different elevations. It can be a bit terse for the new cook. But a few tries will make it pretty clear.

Corbin, Pam and Hugh Fearnley-Whittingstall. *The River Cottage Preserves Handbook.* New York: Ten Speed Press, 2008.

What makes this book so great? A little more exotic take on the science and art of preserving produce.

Kingry, Judi and Lauren Devine, eds. *Complete Book of Home Preserving.* Toronto: Robert Rose, 2006.

What's so great about this book? If you decide you enjoy canning, or end up with more of something than you can handle, and want to do more than just can it plain, look here for more dependable, simple recipes for almost any garden produce you can think of.

EQUIPMENT

f you have the following, you can easily make everything in this cookbook. There is no need to go out and buy anything new if you already have these tools, and no need to buy something really expensive if you don't. Something that is sturdy and well-sized is all you need. Except for the knife, go get a good knife.

Essential equipment: baking sheet, blender, bowls, colander, grater, kitchen towels, knives, measuring cups and spoons, pie pan, plastic cutting board, salad bowl and servers, scrubby brush, snap-top plastic containers, soup pot, spatulas (soft, flat and spreading), vegetable peeler, whisk, and zip-top bags.

Some optional, but really cool equipment that make things easier and/or tastier: salad spinner, spring loaded tongs (love these), grill or cast iron stovetop grill or grill pan, hand blender, food processor, silpat or silicone baking sheet liner, sieve or strainer, and food mill.

I certainly have many more items in my kitchen, but many of them are closer to toys than tools. Some, like a food processor, make things vastly easier when I am dealing with large amounts of food, and others, like cookie cutters, are just fun. However none of them are essential for cooking a super-tasty meal. And you certainly don't need $200 pans and $800 knives. No matter how much you spend, they will not do the cooking for you.

If you need more information about any of these tools, keep reading. These descriptions are only meant to be functional. There are more specific and technical definitions, but this cookbook doesn't care.

baking sheet. A flat metal pan a bit smaller than the baking rack in your oven. Varieties with a small lip around the edge (0.5- to1-inch), like half-sheet pans are the most useful in this cookbook, but a plain flat cookie sheet or large (9 X 13 inches or so) baking pans will do too.

blender. There are times when a knife just can't chop fine enough — or not in the time you have. More buttons does not necessarily mean better, just make sure the one you choose has enough power to crush ice.

bowl. A variety of sizes are useful in any kitchen. There are two sizes you must have to make all these recipes. A large bowl needs to hold 10 to16 cups of stuff. Something large and roomy for mixing and tossing. Stainless steel metal bowls are nice because they are light and unbreakable. A small bowl of 1 or 2 cups in size. Just enough to mix something small, or hold a little bit of something. Cereal, rice, and soup bowls do a great job, as do myriad other random containers.

colander. Get one that is useful for pasta, and it will be useful for just about everything else too. Go ahead and get a sturdy one that will last. A small colander for washing the odd handful of berries is nice, but far from essential.

grater. A sturdy four-sided (box grater) is nice since it provides a solid surface for grating cheese and vegetables. However, very few of us ever use the other three sides. A flat grater with feet that can be placed over a bowl also works well. All you really need is something that won't crumple under pressure.

kitchen towel. A non-fuzzy, cotton, absorbent, large rectangle of cloth, a tea towel. Have many. While good for drying and cleanup, they are invaluable in many other food related areas that paper towels can't manage.

knives. Most kitchens have more knives than we really use. For this cookbook, there are only two sharp knives you really need. Ah yes, and stay away from knives that "never need sharpening," in the end, they will disappoint. And if you aren't ready to teach knife skills to your child, there is one more. In this cookbook, knife means a large (6- to 9-inch blade) all-purpose "chef's" knife. It doesn't have to be expensive (there are good ones out there for around $30), but it must hold an edge well, and feel comfortable in your hand. This is the one item you should test out at a specialty kitchen store. Tell them how much you want to spend, what you want to cook, and make sure you get to test cut with several. Judge by feel, not by fancy knife terms. Using a difficult knife is like wearing shoes that are too small. You won't want to go anywhere. Use a paring knife with a small 3-inch blade for cutting off little bits of stuff (seeds, yucky spots) and paring (peeling) things. For small jobs, it's the only other knife you need for this book. Keep it sharp too. No need for a knife set. (Note: A kid knife is a serrated butter or picnic knife. It only needs to have the ability to cut a cucumber or small zucchini, and it does not require you to keep an eagle eye on it and the kid. Kids can move onto a paring knife when the kid, and you, are ready.)

knife steel (bonus item to be sure). If you learn how to use one while finding the right knife, your relationship with your knife will be smoother, happier, and longer lasting. It hones the knife edge (sort of like a hairbrush shines and neatens hair), and it will keep an edge in good shape if used regularly. But it does not sharpen (just like you need a different tool than a hair brush to actually shorten hair). The knife or cooking store where you purchased your knife will often do that. Skip this for now if it's too much. People can get obsessed with knife trivia.

measuring. Later on, when you have a feel for things, you will get to the point where you can estimate and eyeball ingredients. But beginning cooks get better results by learning what a teaspoon, tablespoon, ¼ C and Cup of ingredients look like and do. And in baking, even the pros measure. Make sure you have a set of measuring cups. Get a sturdy set that can go in the dishwasher, and if you can find it, has the numbers stamped into the material rather than printed on. These may wash off over time and get frustrating for other cooks who are not at the "eye-ball" stage. ¼, $^1/_3$, ½, and 1C are essential. ¾ is nice, but I continue to live without it. Plunger cups, where you pull a plastic sleeve up to the correct amount are handy for liquid and sticky ingredients, but I survived without them for years. Make sure you have a set of measuring spoons. Get the set on a ring. Teaspoons (t or tsp) in sizes ¼, ½, and 1, and a tablespoon (T or Tbs) will get you through. Occasionally you'll find sets with $^1/_8$ tsp (a pinch) and ½ Tbs (1 + ½ tsp), but these are just bonuses, and most of us muddle through without.

pie pan (8, 9 or 10 inches across, and about 1 inch deep). Many materials are fine — metal, glass, ceramic. Just make sure you have one.

plastic cutting board. Get one that is about ¼- to ½-inch (or 1 cm) thick. There are many good cutting boards out there (wood is excellent, but hand wash only), but a plastic one is essential for dealing with raw meats in most homes. It can go in the dishwasher and get squeaky clean. A few other surfaces work fine as well, but I beg you to never use your knife on something it cannot scratch. It will dull your knife so fast you won't know what's happening (glass, I am looking at you).

salad bowl and servers. Having a nice big bowl and a comfortable set of serving utensils you enjoy using make it more likely salads will show up often in your meals, or even as a meal.

saucepan. A deep pan typically used for cooking or heating up to a few cups of liquid. Most come with lids. Usually measured in capacity (a 2-quart pan, a 3-quart pan)

sauté pan. Also a frying pan or a skillet. Any flat, round pan with a 1.5- to 2.5-inch high edge, single long handle, usually about 8- to 12-inches across. Often used for cooking food quickly over higher heats. They come in non-stick, stainless steel, cast iron and many other varieties. Any and all will work. Find one that feels sturdy and has some weight to it, but you can still pick up and shift easily. If you can find one that has a lid or fits a lid you have, it will become more versatile.

scrubby brush. A small stiff bristled brush for cleaning off root vegetables. It does a more thorough job than sponges or towels. And make it a different one than your dish brush.

snap-top plastic containers. Larger ones for storage and leftovers, and smaller ones for mixing up dressing and sauces. They are also extremely nice for giving kids lightweight and unbreakable containers to work with.

soup pot. A tall deep pot in the 8- to10-quart range. Must have a lid to be useful. For making soup, boiling pasta, blanching ingredients, washing toys, etc.

spatula. These come in three varieties. 1. Soft for scraping bowls clean and combining, smoothing and moving around wet or gooey ingredients. 2. Flat for flipping, shifting and stirring ingredients in a hot pan, essential for sautéing. 3. Spreading for an interchangeable tool with a butter knife.

vegetable peeler. Perfect for removing the skin from any solid piece of produce, such as carrots, potatoes, kohlrabi, and so on. Splurge on one with a comfy handle; you'll be using it a whole bunch. The grip handled ones are also easier for kids to use, and making a batch of "carrot noodles" may one day seem like a good idea.

whisk. Get a nice big "balloon" whisk. The smaller ones, while easier to store don't really do the job. The first time you take a full-size whisk to the job of making an omelet, stirring up salad dressing or maybe even stirring up an aioli or mayonnaise (no, not this week, no rush), you'll see that a small whisk with four flimsy wires is actually worse than a fork.

zip-top bags. A handy way to store and marinate produce, and great for limiting air exposure when freezing.

INGREDIENTS

y kitchen is packed with all sorts of crazy stuff, but these are the items I would feel lost without. More importantly they are the background team that drives this cookbook. These are the absolute basics, but if you have them, your options with produce are wide open. And most of these will last practically forever on a shelf or in the fridge:

- broth (in a box or frozen)
- flour
- garlic
- mustard
- oil
- pepper
- salt
- soy sauce
- sugar
- vinegar

If you expand your pantry a bit more with onions, butter, milk, hard cheese, dried yeast, baking powder, baking soda, a few spices such as cinnamon, cayenne pepper or red pepper flakes, coriander, cumin, ground ginger, Italian seasoning, vanilla extract, and a few sauces, like black bean and garlic sauce, chili garlic sauce (sriracha), oyster sauce, the whole book, and so much more, is yours.

SOME TECHNICAL BITS

In the past few years the number of varieties of certain ingredients have exploded. As a kid I had salt, vegetable oil, vinegar, and mustard. Now there are gift sets of "a dozen salts from around the world," entire stores dedicated to olive oils, and cults built around 100-year-old vinegars. Such avalanches of information and selection can be daunting, even intimidating for the cook who just wants to know how to make a strange new bunch of greens tasty in the next twenty minutes.

This section is here to help you sort the hype from the everyday, practical information.

broth/stock. Water infused with tasty flavors by slowly simmering flavorful and aromatic ingredi-

ents in water for long periods of time. Common flavors are chicken, vegetable, beef, and fish. It is simple but time consuming to make, and very easy to buy. These days, broth is available in 1 quart (4 C) boxes in the soup aisle in most grocery stores. Do check the label and make sure all or nearly all the ingredients are food and not chemicals you can't pronounce, and try to get a brand with lower sodium. You can add the salt you want at the end of your recipes. If you do grow into the desire of making your own broth or stock, older American cookbooks like *Joy of Cooking* or the *Fannie Farmer Cookbook* have fairly simple stock recipes, as do most other comprehensive cookbooks.

black bean sauce. One of those intensely flavored Asian condiments that adds yumminess to a dish, but is overpowering when tasted plain. The main flavors are salty and savory. Begin by using the one you can get your hands on most easily — most often in the corner of your local large grocery store where they carry exotic or ethnic ingredients. If you like the results, there are different Korean, Chinese, and Japanese versions, and variation from brand to brand. It can be used in any place you would use soy sauce to give a dish a little flavor boost. Keep in the fridge.

chili-garlic sauce. The popular and most complex sort comes in a squeeze bottle and is called sriracha. This hot sauce, like so many others, comes in an enormous number of varieties. Having a hot sauce handy to add spice to your produce widens the possibilities. Use it as sparingly or generously as suits you. Keep this in your fridge.

emulsifier. A group of ingredients that have the power to get oil and water to mix (for a short or long period of time). Egg yolks classically do this job and are most famous for their role in mayonnaise and Caesar salad, but they can be fussy to work with. Mustard, sour cream, yogurt, miso, and anchovy paste can all do the job too. In this cookbook, you will use emulsifiers to make salad dressings. A great place to experiment.

fats and oil (plain). Fats are the set of big molecules that repel water, feel slippery, carry certain essential vitamins, and keep our cells and organs from leaking and falling apart. Too much is bad news, as is none. Fats that are so refined that we have no idea where they came from are not good for us either. In this cookbook fats will mostly show up as oil, and occasionally, butter. In these recipes, when I simply list "oil" I'm referring to any kind that is stable at high temperatures and has very little flavor. Canola, unfancy olive oil, and vegetable oil will all serve.

oil (extra virgin or cold-pressed). What I mean when I say "tasty oil." The expensive, good stuff. These are specific types of oil that have been squeezed from a particular fruit (like olives), seed (like grape seed) or nut (like walnut) without the aid of heat, steam, or solvents. These oils usually have unique and fragile flavors and are best used in dressings or at the end of recipes. They can be used for sautéing, frying or baking, but that's like wiping a counter with a dress shirt. It'll do the job, but there are more appropriate tools.

mustard. At its most basic, crushed up mustard seeds in liquid. Which seeds, what liquid, and the possibility of other ingredients create the variety. Bright yellow "American" mustard has the spice turmeric added for color and the mellowest flavor. If you're used to one kind, consider experimenting with another. All of them will work in any recipe where "mustard" is mentioned.

oyster sauce. Another mysterious flavor enhancer. Like English Worcestershire sauce, concocted of many odd and exotic ingredients that combine in ways almost impossible to describe. The main flavors are salty and savory, and often shows up in Chinese restaurants paired with broccoli. Begin by using the one you can get your hands on most easily — most often in the corner of your local large grocery store where they carry exotic or ethnic ingredients. Keep this in your fridge.

salt. Sodium chloride, essential for life, but trouble when there's too much of it. (Not enough is no longer a problem in the United States.) Different manufacturing methods create crystals of different shapes. I like using kosher salt just because the crystals are bigger, and I tend to use less since it is easier to feel how much I sprinkle on food. All those fancy salts simply have a few extra substances besides sodium chloride in them to

make the interesting colors and flavors like pink, red, gray, smoked, black, truffle, and so on. In this cookbook, don't worry about it. If someone gives you some fancy salt, try it out, but there is no need to spend time being concerned about it. In this cookbook, and nearly everywhere else, salt is salt.

soy sauce. Also shoyo, tamari. This salty, savory sauce adds depth of flavor to recipes, but should be used sparingly. Look for soy sauce made with ingredients you can pronounce (no acid-hydrolyzed vegetable protein). Tamari is the good stuff and can often be found in wheat free versions. There are even sodium free soy sauces, which still add a savory flavor, but they are hard to find. There is a staggering array of soy sauces out there. Be brave, try something new. Soy sauce need not be refrigerated as it can cause odd crystallization of ingredients.

vinegars and other acids. An enormous family of chemicals identified by the positively charged hydrogen atom hanging off one end. We taste this as sour. Common acids in the kitchen are lemon, lime, orange, and other citrus juices, vinegars, and buttermilk.

vinegar. Acetic acid and flavor. A staggering variety of vinegars are currently available. White vinegar, the simplest, is acetic acid and water. Many cooks claim it is only fit for cleaning. Every other vinegar has its own character. For this cookbook, vinegars are grouped as mild (things with not much flavor, and a gentle acid tang, like rice, cider, or white wine vinegar) or flavorful (things with a very distinct flavor, like balsamic, red wine, champagne, sherry, or Chinese black vinegar). For a sharp or bright acid, citrus juices like lemon and lime are your best bet.

what is it?

PRODUCE IDENTIFICATION GUIDE

leaves
shoots
flowers
fruits
seeds
roots

leaves

Name	Size & Description	Characteristics & Recipes	Quick Idea
arugula	Finger sized, jagged edged greens. Peppery flavor that sometimes leans to bitter.	Good salad accent, bitter flavor mellows when cooked. Green Goddess Salad (p. 10), Hearty Greens (p. 12), Green Rice (p. 18), Arugula Pesto (p. 24)	Make a simple salad of peaches, sweet onion and arugula. Dress with tasty olive oil, vinegar, salt and pepper.
basil HERB	Teardrop shaped shiny green or purple-green leaves. Italian basil is most familiar, purple Thai basil has a stronger anise flavor.	All basils are excellent with vegetables and tart fruits. Green Goddess Salad (p. 10), Green Rice (p. 18), Basic Basil Pesto (p. 22), Herbs Go Everywhere (p. 20), Nectarine Relish (p. 76), A few Bites of Tomato (p. 88)	Try a strawberry, basil, and spinach salad. Dress with tasty olive oil, balsamic vinegar, a sliver of garlic, and salt and pepper.
beet greens	Dark green leaves with red or yellow stems that come on the top of beets.	Nearly indistinguishable from chard. Use the same way. Start With Chard (p. 4), Green Rice (p. 18), Hearty Greens (p. 12)	Slice beet greens and sweet onions into thin ribbons, add a little vinaigrette dressing, and use in a ham or cheese sandwich.
Brussels sprouts	On the stem they look like a club covered with tiny cabbages. Or they can be pulled off the stem and be loose tiny cabbages.	Definite cabbage smell when cooking. Pungent flavor mellows to sweet when cooked. Seasonal Minestrone Soup (p. 98), Roasted Root Vegetables (p. 140), Hearty Greens (p. 12)	Blanch Brussels sprouts whole for 4 minutes (p. 149). Quick cool them in a bowl of half ice, half water. Cut in quarters, and sauté with onions and bacon.
cabbage	Leaves grow in a tight head. Common varieties: GREEN, tight head, smooth light green leaves. PURPLE, tight head, smooth purple leaves. SAVOY, darker green, rough leaves, milder flavor, good for wraps . NAPA, white base, yellow green rough leaves with curly edges, cool flavor. BOK-CHOY OR PAK-CHOY, white sweet flavored base, dark green leaves hold most of the cabbage flavor.	All varieties have a cool flavor with a spicy cabbage bite that mellows to sweet when cooked. Braised Greens with Spicy Sausage (p. 16), Summer Squash (p. 94), Cabbage & Sweet Onion Salad (p. 96), Seasonal Minestrone Soup (p. 98)	Slice into thin ribbons, sauté in a little oil with a pinch of salt, and a sliced onion. Keep cooking until it all softens and turns sweet. Add salt and pepper, a dash of cider vinegar and maybe caraway seeds or sesame oil.

Name	Size & Description	Characteristics & Recipes	Quick Idea
chard	Dark green smooth edged leaves on a thick, crunchy, tender stem. Common varieties: red, pink, yellow, white, and light green.	Leaves have a flat taste that improves with cooking. Start With Chard (p. 4), Hearty Greens (p. 12), Seasonal Minestrone Soup (p. 98)	Raw stems are sweet like celery. Slice them out of the center of the leaves and hand them out as snacks while cooking the leaves. Maybe dip in a little dressing.
chives HERB	Straight and tall and classically green. Mild onion or garlic flavor, depending on the variety.	Herbs Go Everywhere (p. 20), Green Goddess Salad (p. 10), Herb Oils (p. 21), Chive Flower Omelets (p. 60), Herb Roasted Potatoes (p. 131)	Preserve a bounty of chives in butter. Chop chives, add butter (the ratio is 1 part chives to 1 part butter). Roll in plastic wrap. Freeze, slice as needed. (A food processor makes this FAST.)
cilantro	Feathery green leaves have a slightly cool and citrus flavor.	It makes everything spicy or tart even better. Green Rice (p. 18), Herbs Go Everywhere (p. 20), Herb Oils (p. 21), Nectarine & Sweet Onion Relish (p. 76), A Few Bites of Tomato (p. 88)	Chop cilantro, shallots, lime juice, a pinch of salt, and smash with avocado. Guacamole! Adding some chopped tomato is darn tasty too.
collard (greens)	Big, flat, dark green leaves with a waxy sheen and a woody stem. Mild cabbage flavor.	Braise them until soft, but stop before mush. Don't worry, that takes several hours. Hearty Greens (p. 12), Braised Greens with Spicy Sausage (p. 16, Green Rice (p. 18), Seasonal Minestrone Soup (p. 98)	Collard leaf, square of raw fish. Sprinkle with salt and garlic. Grill the fish on the leaf. Gives the fish a smoky note, and no sticking to the grill. Try with a whole fish and bigger leaves.
dill HERB	Long, woody, bright green stems with feathery fronds. Fronds and flowers are the parts typically used as herbs.	Cooling flavor, often used in cucumber pickles. Green Goddess Salad (p. 10), Herbs Go Everywhere(p. 20), Herb Oils (p. 21), Zucchini Pancakes (p. 100), A Few Bites of Tomato (p. 88), Herb Roasted Potatoes (p. 131)	Dill and mint are best friends. Put them together wth apples for a refreshing salad, or with garlic and chopped cucumbers in yogurt for tzatziki.

leaves

Name	Size & Description	Characteristics & Recipes	Quick Idea
endive	Small, cone shaped, with tightly wrapped leaves. White at the base, and light green at the top with fuzzy edges. Slightly bitter.	Pronounced en-dive (or ahn-deev). A Big Green Salad (p. 8), Green Goddess Salad (p. 10), Hearty Greens (p. 12), Fennel Beet & Goat Cheese Salad (p. 138)	Cut in half. Brush on oil or some bacon fat. Grill. Char the flat sides and warm and slightly soften the rest. Drizzle with a little balsamic vinegar and season with salt and pepper.
frisée	Frizzy leaves in a loose head. Either all light green or white in the center with light green tips. Bitter green.	Green Salad (p. 8), Green Goddess Salad (p. 10), Hearty Greens (p. 12), Fennel Beet & Goat Cheese Salad (p. 138)	Good in salads, but add some to hearty greens for cooking. The bitterness mellows and adds sweetness.
kale	Enormous number of colors ranging from black-green to light grey-green. Leaf shapes can be smooth-edged, frilly or ragged looking. Textures can be smooth, waxy or pebbled.	Generally has a tough texture and strong flavor raw that is improved by blanching, roasting, braising or frying. Crispy Kale (p. 6), Hearty Greens (p. 12), Braised Greens with Spicy Sausage (p. 16), Green Rice (p. 18), Seasonal Minestrone Soup (p. 98)	Be bad with your kale. Roll up some and slice into ribbons (chiffonade). Fry in a quarter inch of oil, sprinkle with salt, and put on . . . things.
lemon balm HERB	Heart shaped leaf with rough edges. Slightly fuzzy. Looks like mint, smells like lemon, doesn't taste like much.	Brew as tea or syrup, and add to bouquets for its scent. Herbs Go Everywhere (p. 20), Basil Flower Fizz (p. 53)	As a mint relative, it makes a great tea. In a large glass container, add 4 tea bags, a large handful of leaves, cover and leave in the sun for Lemon Balm Sun Tea.
lemon verbena HERB	Skinny, light green, pointy leaves with a very strong lemon scent.	Not usually eaten raw, usually brewed as tea or syrup, and used in marinades. Herbs Go Everywhere (p. 20), Basil Flower Fizz (p. 53)	Chop lemon verbena, garlic and fresh ginger (ratio is 2 to 1 to 2), pinch of salt, oil to coat. Spread over fish or chicken overnight. Grill or steam (in a collard leaf?).

Name	Size & Description	Characteristics & Recipes	Quick Idea
lettuce	Any tender green leaf with a watery, crunchy center rib, and thin, tender leaves. Comes in head forming and loose leaf varieties. Colors range from light green, to dark green, to red tinged.	Almost always eaten raw, though sweet varieties are excellent in soup or sautéed.	Lettuce wraps. I know they've had their day, but when sweet summer lettuce returns, use it to wrap everything.
lovage HERB	Light yellow green leaves look like celery, and taste very similar. Stalks are hollow.	Ingredient in Roman cuisine. Green Goddess Salad (p. 10), Herbs Go Everywhere (p. 20), Green Rice (p. 18)	Use the hollow stems as straws for summer drinks.
mache	Also corn salad and lamb's lettuce. Thick leaves smaller than palm-sized. Smooth-edged, dark green teardrops. Fresh, mild green flavor.	Use in salads, alone or mixed. Also tasty as a cooked green. A Big Green Salad (p. 8), Green Goddess Salad (p. 10), Seasonal Minestrone Soup (p. 98)	Use as the base of an orange section, radish, and toasted pecan salad with a mild vinaigrette dressing. Goat cheese adds something too.
mint HERB	Round or pointed heart shaped, rough-edged, slightly fuzzy leaves. Common varieties: peppermint, spearmint, lemon mint, chocolate mint, pineapple mint.	Stronger mint flavors are darker green, exotic flavors tend to be lighter green. Green Rice (p. 18), Herbs Go Everywhere (p. 20), Gremolata (p. 26), Herb Oils (p. 21), Pea Shoot Stir Fry (p. 43), Basil Flower Fizz (p. 53), Granita (p. 74), Nectarine and Sweet Onion Relish (p. 76), Minty Peas with Butter (p. 117)	Roll mint leaves and slice into ribbons (chiffonade), stir into soft cheese with a pinch of sugar and salt. Spread on the fruit of the moment.
mizuna	Long, thin, ragged edged dark green leaf with a thick center stem. Has a peppery, hearty flavor.	Typically eaten sautéed or braised. Hearty Greens (p. 12), Braised Greens with Spicy Sausage (p. 16), Green Rice (p. 18), Seasonal Minestrone Soup (p. 98)	Add this spicy hearty green into the last 10 cooking minutes of any soup, stew; or grill or braise with meat. Interesting, in a good way.

Name	Size & Description	Characteristics & Recipes	Quick Idea
mustard greens	Light or dark green, wide, ragged edged leaf. A distinct mustard taste that mellows when braised. Pull large leaves off the woody cylindrical stem.	Serve in small amounts with meats and meaty flavors, or mix with other greens. Hearty Greens (p. 12), Braised Greens with Spicy Sausage (p. 16), Green Rice (p. 18), Seasonal Minestrone Soup (p. 98)	Use the sauté then braise method (p. 17) on a mess of chopped greens. Divide in to spoonfulls. Freeze and store in a zip top bag. Thaw portions to add to dishes that need oomph (omelets, under chicken, in soup, etc.).
nasturtium leaf HERB	Dark green leaves that look like tiny lily pads. A distinct green and spicy flavor.	Usually eaten raw, sliced thin. A Big Green Salad (p. 8), Green Goddess Salad (p. 10), Nasturtium & Sweet Onion Flatbread (p. 52)	Add to any braise to fill out hearty leaves. Cooks down to a tender, sweet leaf from its spicy, raw state.
oregano HERB	Small, teardrop shaped, jagged edged leaf. Often slightly fuzzy. Smells like Italian food, with a slightly resinous flavor.	Green Goddess Salad (p. 8), Herbs Go Everywhere (p. 20), Herb Oils (p. 21), Zucchini Pancakes (p. 100), A Few Bites of Tomato (p. 88), Herb Roasted Potatoes (p. 131)	Sauté spinach with garlic and chopped oregano, stir in salt and lemon zest to balance fried fish and fried chicken. Or stir into noodles.
parsley HERB	Small, dark green, frilly edged leaves on stems that are flat on one side and rounded on the other. Mild, green flavor. Common varieties: flat leaf or Italian, curly.	Green Rice (p. 18), Gremolata (p. 26), Green Goddess Salad (p. 8), Herbs Go Everywhere (p. 20), Herb Oils (p. 21), Herb Roasted Potatoes (p. 131)	Parsley plays nice with all the other herbs. If you have some, add a bit to whatever else you are using. Though common, it also plays the role of secret ingredient.
rosemary HERB	Extremely skinny leaves that look and smell a bit like pine needles.	Almost always a cooked herb. Herbs Go Everywhere (p. 20), Herb Oils (p. 21), Herb Roasted Potatoes (p. 131)	Make rosemary simple syrup (p. 21). Use as the base for rosemary lemonade (add limoncello for the adult version).

Name	Size & Description	Characteristics & Recipes	Quick Idea
sage HERB	Fuzzy, light grey-green leaves, usually an elongated teardrop shape in a range of sizes.	Resinous flavor when raw, but adds a pleasant savory flavor when cooked. Herb Oils (p. 21), Roasted Root Vegetables (p. 140), Herb Roasted Potatoes (p. 131)	Fry sage leaves in oil, sprinkle over lemon garlic chicken.
savory HERB	Tiny dark green leaves that taste and look similar to thyme.	Adds excellent flavor to beans and other vegetables. Gremolata (p. 26), Green Goddess Salad (p. 8), Herbs Go Everywhere (p. 20), Herb Oils (p. 21), Oven Roasted Green Beans (p. 112), Beans, Bacon & Summer Savory (p. 114), Herb Roasted Potatoes (p. 131)	Throw in the pot when cooking dried beans to add flavor. Chop up a few fresh leaves into the dish that is using the beans.
sorrel HERB	Large teardrop shaped leaf. Light yellow-green and super duper sour. Shows up early in the spring.	Famous as cream of sorrel soup. A Big Green Salad (p. 8), Green Goddess Salad (p. 10), Green Rice (p. 18)	Toss into the blender with smoothie ingredients. The sour flavor perks up everything, and the vitamins are pretty awesome too.
spinach	Dark green, very tender leaf. Comes in baby and mature sizes. Chinese spinach or Indian spinach are usually amaranth leaves, but are completely interchangeable.	Raw leaves have a mild bitter taste that can become more so when cooked. Add vinegar or blanch to chase it away. Green Rice (p. 18), Hearty Greens (p. 12), Braised Greens with Spicy Sausage (p. 16), Green Rice (p. 18), Seasonal Minestrone Soup (p. 98)	If you got some beautiful meat from the Farmers Market, render off a bit of the fat, and use that as the base to sauté the spinach for unexpected, deep, round flavors.
tarragon HERB	Thin, pointed, light green leaves on a woody stem have a vaguely anise scent mixed with mysterious green flavors.	Excellent flavor to add to vegetable, chicken and fish dishes. Green Goddess Salad (p. 8), Herbs Go Everywhere (p. 20), Herb Oils (p. 21)	Pureé tarragon with oil (ratio of 2 to 1). Stir a little into a few Tbs mayo for tarragon mayonnaise. Another time, make mayonnaise from scratch.

leaves

Name	Size & Description	Characteristics & Recipes	Quick Idea
thyme HERB	Teeny leaves on a woody stem. Smells like all the other herbs mixed together. Lemon thyme does live up to its name.	Herbs Go Everywhere (p. 20), Green Rice (p. 18), Gremolata (p. 26), Herb Oils (p. 21), Nectarine and Sweet Onion Relish (p. 76), Herb Roasted Potatoes (p. 131)	Be sure to try a thyme vinaigrette. Toss some leaves into any dressing to give it fresh herbal flavor.
turnip greens	Bright green leaves on top of very fresh turnips. Can resemble arugula, mustard greens, or kale. Slightly spicy flavor that mellows with cooking.	Hearty Greens (p. 12), Braised Greens with Spicy Sausage (p. 16), Green Rice (p. 18)	As a cabbage cousin, turnip greens can stand in for or accompany cooked cabbage. Wrap around a shrimp or a slice of chicken and steam.

Name	Size & Description	Characteristics & Recipes	Quick Idea
asparagus	Green with tightly closed greenish-purple buds at their pointy tips. Range in size from pencil thin to thicker than your thumb.	Peel the thickest ones. Roasted Asparagus (p. 36), Raw Asparagus Salad (p. 38)	Stir lemon juice and zest (and parsley) into some mayonnaise for enviable asparagus dipping sauce.
broccoli	Traditional crown broccoli has lighter green thick stems, and a tree-top of dark green tightly closed buds. Other varieties tend to have darker green stems ranging from pencil to thumb thickness with small clusters of buds at the base of ripple-edged dark green leaves. All broccolis have a similar flavor, though the smaller varieties are often milder.	Common varieties: Chinese broccoli, gai-lan or kai-lan, broccoli rabe, rapini. Tight buds bloom into tiny yellow flowers that smell just like broccoli and are fun to add to salads. Black Bean and Garlic Kohlrabi (p. 42), Blanched Kohlrabi Marinated in Oil (p. 40), Artichoke Stems, Parmesan & Grains (p. 48)	Cut an inch off the bottom of one stem of broccoli. Put it in water just to see (and smell, and taste) the flowers.
cardoon	It looks like celery covered with grey dust and prickles. It is believed to be the proto-artichoke.	Artichoke Stems, Parmesan & Grains (p. 48), Artichoke Petals & Lemon Garlic Dressing (p. 56)	If you find someone selling it, ask them for their favorite recipe. I bet it is amazing. Lacking that, clean, tempura batter, and fry. Eat with lemons and white wine. Thank me later, after the scratches have healed.
celery	Tall, light green bunched stalks. The light green leaves inside are sweet, tingly, and tasty.	The intensely flavored red variety is best for flavoring stocks and soup. A Big Green Salad (p. 8), Green Goddess Salad (p. 10), Seasonal Minestrone Soup (p. 98)	Slice into thin crescent moons. Add thin slices of apple and mint. Make an oil and vinegar dressing with celery seed, garlic, and salt and pepper.
garlic scape	Smooth, light green stalk with pointed bud on top. Mild, sweet garlic flavor.	Slightly woody texture when raw, best cooked. Garlic Scapes (p. 44), Roasted Asparagus (p. 36), Hearty Greens (p. 12)	Slice the scapes. Fry 'em up. Then fry bread crumbs with salt and red pepper flakes. Toss with pasta (and maybe some sausage).

shoots

Name	Size & Description	Characteristics & Recipes	Quick Idea
kohlrabi	Bright green-yellow color. A waxy skin over a crunchy flesh with a potato-meets-apple texture and a sweet, watery broccoli flavor.	Can be eaten raw. Older, tougher, stored specimens have a stronger taste and should be cooked. Black Bean and Garlic Kohlrabi (p. 42), Blanched Kohlrabi Marinated in Oil (p. 40)	Grate fresh, sweet kohlrabi with carrots. Toss with soy, garlic, rice vinegar, sesame seeds (and sriracha if you like spicy) for a quick slaw.
leek	Looks like a giant green onion. White base, light green middle and darker green tops. Very mild onion flavor.	White and light green part is generally eaten cooked. Melted Leeks (p. 46)	Baby (early) leeks grill like a dream alongside the other thing you are grilling. Drizzle with an herby vinaigrette.
onion scape	Hollow striped stalk with a ball bud at the top.	Green onion taste and texture, eat raw or cooked. Chive Flower Omelet (p. 60), A Big Green Salad (p. 8), A Few Bites of Tomato (p. 88)	Use instead of green onions, and chop up the bloom for flair. A natural over omelets, quiches, and other egg things.
pea shoots	Tender tips of a pea plant, usually has 2 to 6 leaves and some curly tendrils. Tastes like pea pods. Associated flowers are also edible.	Edible raw or lightly cooked. Pea Shoot Stir Fry (p. 43), Green Goddess Salad (p. 10), Hearty Greens (p. 12), Green Rice (p. 18)	If you have extra pea seeds, keep growing shoots. Chop them with mint, parsley, thyme, and garlic. Smash into butter and spread on bread for a late spring surprise.

Name	Size & Description	Characteristics & Recipes	Quick Idea
artichoke	Looks like the egg of a green, dinosaur sized pangolin or armadillo. The base of each leaf has a mysterious sweet and savory flavor. Scoop out the fuzzy bit (the choke) with a spoon.	The stem is tasty too, but it needs to be peeled. Artichoke Petals & Lemon Garlic Dressing (p. 56), Artichoke Stems, Parmesan & Grains Salad (p. 48), Roasted Asparagus (p. 36)	Cheat. Buy marinated artichoke hearts. Chop them, sauté in some of their juices with chopped onions, stir in some ricotta and herbs. Top some pasta. Or make your own marinated artichoke hearts. See the Oil Marinade recipe (p. 40).
arugula flower	Nickel sized white flower with dark stripes that show up when arugula gets too much sun. They have a mild spicy flavor with a mysterious sweetness. Some claim they taste vaguely of peanuts.	When you get them, enjoy them by tossing them in salads, on omelets, and eating plain. Big Green Salad (p. 8), Arugula Flower Garlic Bread (p. 59), Chive Flower Omelet (p. 60), Nectarine and Sweet Onion Relish (p. 76), Fruits Love Cheeses (p. 77)	When you start to get flowers, cut the stems and pop them in water. Then as you serve up salads a few days later, surprise family and friends by decorating the salads with flowers.
borage	The other blue food. A star shaped flower that tastes faintly of cucumbers, as do the leaves and stem.	Add this flower to salads and summer drinks. Green Goddess Salad (p. 10), Basil Flower Fizz (p. 53), Arugula Flower Garlic Bread (p. 59), Nectarine & Sweet Onion Relish (p. 76)	Make double thick sugar syrup (2 C sugar and 1 C water), bring to a boil and cool. Coat wax paper in super fine sugar. Dip flowers in syrup, place on the sugar lined paper. Let dry overnight. Use to be fancy.
cauliflower	A cabbage relative with cabbage flavor. Light green leaves surround a tight, hard head (curd) of proto-flowers. Comes in white, yellow, green, and purple.	The green-yellow Romanesco variety looks like a math problem. Roasted Asparagus (p. 36), Blanched Kohlrabi Marinated in Oil (p. 40), Seasonal Minestrone Soup (p. 98), Roasted Root Vegetables (p. 140)	Marinate thick slices in yogurt seasoned with cumin, salt, and mustard. Brown in a saute pan. Sprinkle with cilantro and/or parsley.
chive flower	A light purple ball sitting at the top of a chive. If a garlic or onion scape blooms, it will look like a giant version of this. It has a gentle onion or garlic flavor, depending on the type of chive, laced with a little sweetness from the nectar at the base of each little purple spear.	The subtle flavor of chive flowers is best eaten raw. They go great in salads, and are a super garnish for any dish with onion. Big Green Salad (p. 8), Green Goddess Salad (p. 10), Flatbread with Herb Oils and Leftovers (p. 32), Raw Asparagus Salad (p. 38), Arugula Flower Garlic Bread (p. 59), Chive Flower Omelet (p. 60), Nectarine & Sweet Onion Relish (p. 76), Fava Beans in Garlicky Dressing (p. 120)	Crispy fried chive flowers. If you end up with lots of chive flowers, heat about a half-inch of oil in a small sauce pan to 275 – 300° F. Lower the flowers in the hot oil with a slotted spoon. Fry until the flowers are an even dark purple (around 10 seconds). Surprise your friends.

Name	Size & Description	Characteristics & Recipes	Quick Idea
marigold	Bright gold pom-pom of a flower. The petals have a slightly bitter, peppery flavor.	Add to salads or compound butter. Green Rice (p. 18), Arugula Pesto (p. 24), Chive Flower Omelets (p. 60), Arugula Flower Garlic Bread (p. 59), Fennel, Beet & Goat Cheese Salad (p. 138)	Tastes of mild radishes. Sprinkle over burritos, nachos, tacos, or quesadillas.
nasturtium	Five petaled cup shaped flower with a horn on the back. This is where most of the spicy flavor lies; yellow, orange, red, white and pink.	Nasturtium & Sweet Onion Flatbread (p. 52), Arugula Flower Garlic Bread (p. 59), A Big Green Salad (p. 8), Green Goddess Salad (p. 10), Nectarine & Sweet Onion Relish (p. 76)	Go ahead and try one. Spicy with a hint of sweet. Then share with your children and friends. Belongs with onions and savory flavors.
pansy	Purple, pink, white or yellow flowers that look like a chubby face. A slightly minty, sweet flavor.	Eaten in salads, and on desserts. A big Green Salad (p. 8), Green Goddess Salad (p. 10), Granita (p. 74), Basil Flower Fizz (p. 53)	Grind petals in a food processor 1 to 1 with granulated sugar to make flower paste. Use to make sweet compound butter or syrup
rose	Range from white to red, culinary roses are usually pink. Adds fragrance and a mildly bitter taste.	Common in Persian food, desserts, and occasionally, tea. Basil Flower Fizz (p. 53), Granita (p. 74)	Make flower paste to create a sweet fragrant butter or syrup. Use with a light hand — this is strong stuff.
squash blossom	Large yellow flower with a large center part (the pistil or stamen) that is usually removed before cooking or eating. Has a vaguely summer squash flavor	Can be summer or winter squash. Squash Blossom Pancakes (p. 54), A Big Green Salad (p. 8)	Ambitious? Look up a recipe for stuffed, fried squash blossoms. Otherwise, slice thin and include in salads or with eggs.

Name	Size & Description	Characteristics & Recipes	Quick Idea
acorn squash	Softball to cantaloupe sized. Dark green with small to large yellow splotches and mildly stringy yellow-orange flesh.	Mild squash flavor, in need of salt and seasoning. Baked Delicata Squash (p. 106), Mexican Chocolate Zucchini Bread (p. 104)	Cut into wedges. Toss with salt and oil. Bake at 425°F until soft. Toss in an herb and garlic vinaigrette and serve over braised greens. (Secret: Do this ahead and freeze them. Thaw later over braised greens.)
apple	Hundreds of varieties colored green to yellow to pink to red. Flavor ranges from pucker-sour to dessert-sweet.	Ask your farmer which is which. Take a bite and enjoy! A Big Green Salad (p. 8), Fruits Love Cheeses (p. 77), Granita (p. 74), Applesauce (p. 82), Smoothies (p. 84)	Peel and cut into thin slices, cut those to matchsticks. Toss with mint and basil. Dress with olive oil, cider vinegar, salt, and pepper. Wrap in a lettuce leaf with shrimp, crab, or fish.
apricot	Delicate orange with a hint of pink, tender and fuzzy. Easily cupped in the palm of your hand.	Ripe when flesh is soft to a gentle poke, but not squishy. Stone Fruit Cake (p. 66), Clafouti (p. 68), Summer Berry Pie Bars (p. 72), Granita (p. 74), Fruits Love Cheeses (p. 77), Ginger Shortbread & Stone Fruits (p. 78), Fruit Scones (p. 80), Applesauce (p. 82), Smoothies (p. 84)	After you eat some plain, slice over ice cream, yogurt, or eat with soft cheeses. Excellent with almonds and cashews. Try frozen slices with mint.
aprium	Usually apricot colored, but not fuzzy. Firmer, tarter version of the apricot, crossed with a plum.	Use like a plum or an apricot. Eat when barely soft and smells amazing. A Big Green Salad (p. 8), Stone Fruit Cake (p. 66), Baked Ginger Pluots (p. 67), Nectarine & Sweet Onion Relish (p. 76), Clafouti (p. 68), Summer Berry Pie Bars (p. 72), Granita (p. 74), Fruits Love Cheeses (p. 77), Ginger Shortbread & Stone Fruits (p. 78), Fruit Scones (p. 80), Smoothies (p. 84)	Slice and freeze the ones that are ripening too fast. Use in smoothies with early sorrel, orange juice, and maybe a little yogurt or tofu.
blackberry	Thumb sized berries made of little purple-black drops. Sweetest when they turn dull, are no longer shiny, and smell like blackberries.	Rich sweet flavor and heady scent. Clafouti (p. 68), Summer Berry Pie Bars (p. 72), Granita (p. 74), Fruit Scones (p. 80), Smoothies (p. 84)	Lettuce salad with blackberries, sweet onions, grilled pork loin, and citrus, blackberry, vinaigrette dressing. Summer Supper of Excellence.

Name	Size & Description	Characteristics & Recipes	Quick Idea
blueberry	Blue. The darker the better, with a funny little crown opposite the stem. Range in size from pinky-nail to thumb-nail.	Smaller berries are more intense and tart; larger berries are sweeter. Clafouti (p. 68), Summer Berry Pie Bars (p. 72), Granita (p. 74), Fruit Scones (p. 80), Smoothies (p. 84)	In or on pancakes or waffles. Fresh or frozen. That is where blueberries belong.
butternut squash	Tan or pale-yellow hard squash. Bulb at the bottom, skinnier neck at the top. Bright orange flesh inside. One of the smoothest, least stringy squashes.	Texture is closer to cooked sweet potato than pumpkin. Baked Delicata Squash (p. 106), Mexican Chocolate Zucchini Bread (p. 104), Sweet & Spicy Butternut Squash Soup (p. 108), Roasted Root Vegetables (p. 140)	Cut off the neck, peel, cut into thin slices, toss with oil and salt, roast at about 425°F until tender. Sprinkle with citrus juice, and paprika.
cantaloupe	Also musk melon. Anything with a green or orange base covered by a tan colored rough net fall into this muskmelon group. New hybrids are appearing all the time.	Ripe when it smells melony, feels heavy, and is no longer rock hard where the stem broke off. Granita (p. 74), Smoothies (p. 84)	A perfectly ripe slice of melon and a thin slice of salty ham, prosciutto or salty blue cheese is a classic. Will beat the pants off of any version you had in a restaurant.
cherry	The smallest stone fruit. Best on the stem, ready to eat when the shiny skin is firm, but gives to pressure. Sweet varieties include Bing (dark red) and Rainier (yellow with red patches). Sour or pie-cherries include Montmorency.	Sweet cherries are ready to eat, but pie cherries need to be cooked with sugar. The flavor is worth the trouble. Stone Fruit Cake (p. 66), Baked Ginger Pluots (p. 67), Clafouti (p. 68), Summer Berry Pie Bars (p. 72), Granita (p. 74), Fruits Love Cheeses (p. 77), Ginger Shortbread & Stone Fruits (p. 78), Fruit Scones (p. 80)	Pit the cheries, blend, then strain. Add the juice to sparkling water for a cool summer surprise. Sweet or "pie" cherries are both pleasing this way. (The juice freezes for later too!)
chili pepper	Also hot peppers. They come in a menagerie of sizes and a rainbow of colors. Usually a green stem, and round shoulders that taper to a pointy end. Common Varieties: Serrano, jalapeño, Anaheim, aji, banana, pasilla, pablano, bell.	Rule of thumb; smaller is hotter, bigger is milder. Always ask because there are plenty of exceptions. Green Rice (p. 18), Herb Oils (p. 21), Nectarine & Sweet Onion Relish (p. 76), A Few Bites of Tomato (p. 88), Grilled Cheese & Tomato Sandwich (p. 93), Zucchini Pancakes (p. 100)	Candied peppers: 1 C cider vinegar, 2 C sugar, ½ tsp salt. Bring to a boil. 8 oz. peppers, cut off stems. Cut in ¼ slices. Add to syrup. Simmer 5 minutes. Cool, store in fridge almost forever. Or make it with water, but it won't last quite as long. On hot days, add to a glass of ice water and cucumber or watermelon slices.

Name	Size & Description	Characteristics & Recipes	Quick Idea
cucumber	Thin green skin, watery white or pale green flesh. Extremely cooling to eat, with a slightly sweet flavor. Range in size from large-finger to forearm sized. Yellow ball shaped lemon cucumber, tastes like a cucumber, alas, not at all lemony.	Sometimes have defensive prickles that are easily washed off under water. Typically bumpy skin varieties are pickling and smooth skinned are salad or slicing types. All are good raw. A Big Green Salad (p. 8), Green Goddess Salad (p. 10), Nasturtium & Sweet Onion Flat Bread (p. 52), A Few Bites of Tomato (p. 88), Summer Squash & Sweet Onion Salad (p. 96), Sesame Soy Zucchini (p. 103)	Make cucumber syrup for fizzy drinks. ½ C water, 1½ C sugar, 2 C cucumber chopped fine. Boil sugar and water. Take off heat, add cucumber, cool, refridgerate. Strain to use. On hot days, refrigerate water with cucumber slices. Tasty! Or make cucumber agua fresca (see honeydew melon).
delicata squash	Small, football shaped hard squash. Light yellow skin with white and orange or green stripes. Orange flesh is very smooth, almost interchangeable with sweet potato.	Also known as sweet potato squash. Baked Delicata Squash (p. 106), Sweet & Spicy Butternut Squash Soup (p. 108), Roasted Root Vegetables (p. 140)	Cut off the ends, peel. Scoop the seeds out of the center and slice into rounds. Simmer in butter until soft. Make sure to use salt and pepper. Add to salad for an amazing combination.
eggplant	Thin shiny skin and light green spiky cap of leaves. Typically thinner at the stem end and swells towards the base. Purple or green or white or a combination of two of the three colors. Spongy white flesh with small yellow or grey edible seeds. Common varieties: Japanese, green, ball, purple, graffiti, white, pea.	Needs significant cooking to soften flesh. Skin is edible, but is often peeled. Blanched Kohlrabi Marinated in Oil (p. 40), Roasted Root Vegetables (p. 140)	Cut eggplant in half. Brush with oil. Grill face down to get a smoky flavor, then flip and cook 'til shriveled and very soft. Scoop out flesh into the blender. Add a little salt, lemon juice, garlic and tahini. Top with good olive oil. Baba Ganoush!
honeydew melon	Green smooth skin, ball shaped. Flesh can be light green, white, or tinged orange. Lots of new hybrids.	Flavor is honey sweet and watery. The stem end will smell sweet when it is ripe. Granita (p. 74), Smoothies (p. 84)	Agua fresca. Pop a handful of peeled slices in a blender with a splash of water, 1 or 2 ice cubes, maybe a little sugar. Blend. Sip on a hot day.
kabocha squash	Dark green softball or larger sized hard squash, with a slightly smooshed shape. Some have a few yellow blotches. Bright orange flesh.	The smooth flesh of this squash can smell faintly of apricots. Baked Delicata Squash(p. 106), Mexican Chocolate Zucchini Bread (p. 104), Sweet & Spicy Butternut Squash Soup (p. 108), Roasted Root Vegetables (p. 140), Herb Roasted Potatoes (p. 131)	When baking squash, bake lots and freeze mashed squash in measured amounts for easy use later.

fruits

Name	Size & Description	Characteristics & Recipes	Quick Idea
marionberry	Looks like a lighter purple-red blackberry and is another blackberry cross. Ripe when still shiny.	Less sweet than blackberries, but equally excellent flavor. Big Green Salad (p. 8), Clafouti (p. 68), Summer Berry Pie Bars (p. 72), Granita (p. 74), Fruit Scones (p. 80), Smoothies (p. 84)	Mini cobbler (see peach). Fill with berries and proceed.
nectarine	Baseball sized fruit with a smooth orange-pink skin and a red blush. Tart peachy flavor.	Ripe when flesh gives to gentle pressure and smells delicious. A Big Green Salad (p. 8), Stone Fruit Cake (p. 66), Baked Ginger Pluots (p. 67), Clafouti (p. 68), Nectarine & Sweet Onion Relish (p. 76), Summer Berry Pie Bars (p. 72), Granita (p. 74) Fruits Love Cheeses (p. 77), Ginger Shortbread & Stone Fruits (p. 78), Fruit Scones (p. 80), Smoothies (p. 84)	Excellent baked, and keeps a touch of its tart taste. See peach and pear.
peach	Baseball sized fruit with a fuzzy orange-pink skin and a red blush. Sweet, juicy, unique flavor.	Ripe when flesh gives to gentle pressure and it smells delicious. A Big Green Salad (p. 8), Stone Fruit Cake (p. 66), Baked Ginger Pluots (p. 67), Clafouti (p. 68), Nectarine & Sweet Onion Relish (p. 76), Summer Berry Pie Bars (p. 72), Granita (p. 74), Fruits Love Cheeses (p. 77), Ginger Shortbread & Stone Fruits (p. 78), Fruit Scones (p. 80), Smoothies (p. 84)	Mini cobbler. Oven safe mug or bowl. Fill with cut fruit, add 1 Tbs sugar, pat butter, pinch of orange zest and salt. Cover with pie crust or sweet biscuit. Bake 350°F or until fruit collapses and the crust is done.
pear	Swollen base tapers to a point with a hard, brown stem. Thin smooth skin covers white grainy flesh. Ripe pears are usually yellow, yellow-green, reddish or brown.	Some varieties are enjoyed crisp; Asian pears (actually apple shaped), Bartlett, Red. Others are eaten soft, when the flesh around the stem softens and gives under gentle pressure; Bartlett, Bosc, Forelle, Comice, Seckel. A Big Green Salad (p. 8), Baked Ginger Pluots (p. 67), Granita (p. 74), Fruits Love Cheeses (p. 77), Applesauce (p. 82), Smoothies (p. 84)	Pear toast. Thin slices of pear on bread and butter. Top with cinnamon sugar. Toast until pear is soft.
plum	Golf ball sized or larger. Smooth skinned and they come in a range of colors from yellow-green, to red, to purple and many in between. The flesh may match the skin or be a surprising contrast.	Ripe plums smell sweet, and give to gentle pressure. The best ones make a juicy mess when eaten. A Big Green Salad (p. 8), Stone Fruit Cake (p. 66), Baked Ginger Pluots (p. 67), Clafouti (p. 68), Nectarine & Sweet Onion Relish (p. 76), Summer Berry Pie Bars (p. 72), Granita (p. 74), Fruits Love Cheeses (p. 77), Ginger Shortbread & Stone Fruits (p. 78), Fruit Scones (p. 80), Smoothies (p. 84)	Go savory. Cook down plums with sliced onions, and salt and pepper, until they are soft and rich. Use to top pork or lamb in place of applesauce.

Name	Size & Description	Characteristics & Recipes	Quick Idea
pluot	Cross of a plum and apricot. Smooth skinned, fits in the palm of your hand. Usually pinky-red.	Ripe pluots gives to a gentle poke, and smell delicious. A Big Green Salad (p. 8), Stone Fruit Cake (p. 66), Baked Ginger Pluots (p. 67), Clafouti (p. 68), Nectarine & Sweet Onion Relish (p. 76), Summer Berry Pie Bars (p. 72), Granita (p. 74), Fruits Love Cheeses (p. 77), Ginger Shortbread & Stone Fruits (p. 78), Fruit Scones (p. 80), Smoothies (p. 84)	Use like plums, nectarines, or apricots.
pumpkin	Typically orange, with a slightly flattened ball shape. All have orange flesh that is more or less stringy. Smaller ones usually have better taste and texture, larger ones are better for carving.	All are great for harvesting the seeds to roast. Some oddballs include white or ghost pumpkins. Also look for blue and warty specimens. Baked Delicata Squash (p. 106), Mexican Chocolate Zucchini Bread (p. 104), Sweet & Spicy Butternut Squash Soup (p. 108), Roasted Pumpkin Seeds (p. 126), Roasted Root Vegetables (p. 140)	Cut open, scoop out the seeds, and peel. Grate with potatoes and onions. Sauté to soften and brown all the ingredients to make a hash. Be sure to season with salt and pepper.
raspberry	Small, cone shaped fruit made of reddish, barely purple drops.	Sweet flavor with a tiny hint of sour. The best berries are very fragile. Eat, use, or freeze immediately. Clafouti (p. 68), Summer Berry Pie Bars (p. 72), Granita (p. 74), Fruit Scones (p. 80), Smoothies (p. 84)	A friend to mint. Chop some mint, smash with raspberries and a little simple syrup. Stir into yogurt and freeze for an ice pop, or add fizzy water for a special summer drink.
strawberry	Red heart shaped fruit with a green crown and seeds on the outside. Eat, make jam, freeze, or refrigerate immediately.	The very best ones collapse in your mouth with a sweet, tart, uniquely strawberry flavor. Granita (p. 74), Strawberry Butter (p. 69), Smoothies (p. 84)	Mix 1 Tbs brown sugar and a dribble of Grand Marnier liqueur into ½ C sour cream or thick yogurt or Mascarpone cheese. Dip strawberries and only share with people who have been nice to you.
tomato	Not just red anymore. Size ranges from grape to cherry to plum to baseball and larger. Some are many lobed and irregular. Shiny smooth skin with matching flesh. Spaces inside contain edible green seeds encased in jelly. Colors include purple, red, orange, yellow, and green.	Yellow and orange are typically sweeter, purple and green often have a bit less tomato taste. All are ripe when their flesh gives to gentle pressure, and they exude a green scent. A Few Bites of Tomato (p. 88), Toasted Tomato Sandwich (p. 90), Grilled Cheese & Tomato Sandwich (p. 93), Seasonal Minestrone Soup (p. 98), Fava Beans in Garlicky Dressing (p. 120), Nasturtium & Sweet Onion Flatbread (p. 52), Herb Oils & Flatbread (p. 32)	Take all the ugly tomatoes and the ones about to go over to the dark side. Blend or chop them small. Wrap in a kitchen towel and hang overnight over a bowl. Tomato water. Ta-da! (Use or freeze the water for later use.) I may or may not have used this for a Bloody Mary.

Name	Size & Description	Characteristics & Recipes	Quick Idea
watermelon	Green skinned with white stripes and typically bright pink flesh. Range in size from softball to toddler. Ripe ones feel heavy for their size and sound hollow when thumped.	New hybrids appear all the time, including yellow and white. Granita (p. 74), Smoothies (p. 84)	Cut extra watermelon into cubes. Spread out on a tray and freeze. Use as ice cubes. Or make agua fresca (see honeydew melons), spike with candied peppers. Or make watermelon water (see tomatoes).
yellow summer squash	Also crookneck squash and patty pan squash. Any shape squash with thin yellow skin and white, slightly spongy flesh. Ranges in size from golf ball to table leg. Smaller than your forearm is best. Interchangeable with zucchini. Common varieties: ball, crookneck, patty pan, zephyr, banana.	Sometimes there will be small prickles on the skin that are easily washed off under water. Blanched Kohlrabi Marinated in Oil (p. 40), Oven Roasted Summer Squash (p. 94), Summer Squash, Cabbage & Sweet Onion Salad (p. 96), Seasonal Minestrone Soup (p. 98), Sesame Soy Zucchini (p. 103), Zucchini Pancakes (p. 100), Mexican Chocolate Zucchini Bread (p. 104)	Honestly, it is zucchini of a different color. See below.
zucchini	Thin-skinned dark green, or green and white squash with white, slightly spongy flesh. Ranges in size from thumb-size (with blossom) to table leg. Smaller than your forearm is best. Interchangeable with yellow summer squash.	Sometimes there will be small prickles on the skin that are easily washed off under water. Blanched Kohlrabi Marinated in Oil (p. 40), Oven Roasted Summer Squash (p. 94), Summer Squash, Cabbage & Sweet Onion Salad (p. 96), Seasonal Minestrone Soup (p. 98), Sesame Soy Zucchini (p. 103), Zucchini Pancakes (p. 100), Mexican Chocolate Zucchini Bread (p. 104)	Deep fry thin slices. Let cool as little as possible. Serve with salt and pepper. Even better, use some of that fancy salt you got as a gift.

Name	Size & Description	Characteristics & Recipes	Quick Idea
canned beans	An excellent pantry staple. Great for boosting soups and salads into meal territory. Common Varieties: red, kidney, cannellini, white, Navy, black, garbanzo, pinto.	Try a new variety, and find your favorite. A Big Green Salad (p. 8), Seasonal Minestrone Soup (p. 98), Beans, Bacon & Summer Savory (p. 114), Fava Beans in Garlicky Dressing (p. 120)	Any-Bean-Dip. Drain, dump into the blender. Add the juice of a lemon or lime, pinch of salt, handful of herbs. Blend until smooth. Adjust for salt, sour , herbs and oil for creaminess.
chick pea	Also garbanzo beans. Green ones come in fuzzy, swollen bright green pods. May appear at a farmers market. Fully mature, they are tan,usually canned, sometimes dried.	To eat green ones, remove the shell, and the thin skin that covers each individual bean. Cook like fava beans. A Big Green Salad (p. 8), Seasonal Minestrone Soup (p. 98), Fava Beans in Garlicky Dressing (p. 120)	Fastest Hummus. 14.5 oz. can of chick peas. Drain ½ way. Pour into blender. Add 1 spoon tahini, squeeze of lemon, handful of parsley, pinch salt, 1 clove garlic. Turn on the blender. Slowly pour in olive oil until it is smooth.
corn	Buy with the stringy silk and green husks on. Look inside for firm, plump, yellow or white kernels.	Other colors may appear at your market. A Big Green Salad (p. 8), Nectarine & Sweet Onion Relish (p. 76), Quickest Sweet Corn (p. 122), Grilled Corn on the Cob (p. 125), Seasonal Minestrone Soup (p. 98)	Use in the Green Rice Recipe for a Japanese and Central American favorite
edamame	Also green soy beans. Firm, fuzzy, light green seed pods. Inside are bright green beans with a thin green skin.	Cook like fava beans. Remove from pod and thin skin. A Big Green Salad (p. 8), Seasonal Minestrone Soup (p. 98), Fava Beans in Garlicky Dressing (p. 120)	Boil pods in salted water for 5 to 10 minutes. Peel out of the pod and inner skin. Eat as a snack warm or cool.
English peas	Also garden peas. Thick, swollen, bright green pods with round peas inside.	Pods are not edible, but no second skin to peel. Seasonal Minestrone Soup (p. 98), Minty Peas with Butter (p. 117), Green Rice (p. 18), Arugula Pesto (p. 24)	Heat 3 Tbs butter to bubbling in a skillet with a generous pinch of salt. Roll the peas around over the heat until they look shiny and wrinkled. Salty, sweet, buttery peas.

Name	Size & Description	Characteristics & Recipes	Quick Idea
fava beans	Light green, large, padded, slightly fuzzy pods.	Beans inside are bright green covered by a light green skin that also needs to be removed. Grilled Fava Beans (p. 118), Fava Beans in Garlicky Dressing (p. 120), Beans, Bacon & Summer Savory (p. 114)	I confess, fava beans are not quick. Grill 'em, boil 'em, steam 'em (see recipes) but you gotta peel 'em, and that takes time. But, they are worth the trouble.
green beans	Green seed pod, finger length or longer, but much slimmer. Comes in yellow, speckley and purple as well.	Pod is edible, in fact, that is the point. These are very immature versions of canned beans and dried beans. Seasonal Minestrone Soup (p. 98), Oven Roasted Green Beans (p. 112), Beans, Bacon & Summer Savory (p. 114), Blanched Kohlrabi Marinated in Oil (p. 40), Artichoke Stems, Parmesan and Grains Salad (p. 48)	Boil water, blanch for 2 minutes. Stop the cooking by straining and dropping into ice water. Use in crudité/veggie tray. Make that lemony mayonnaise for Asparagus (p. 36), or use Green Goddess Dressing (p. 10).
shell beans	Any bean that comes in a pod that must be removed before eating it.	New World beans (like green beans) have no inner skin. These are shell beans when fully mature and harvested for the seeds. Old World types must have their pods removed whether immature or fully mature. They also have a thin skin around each seed that should also be removed. Examples are edamame, fava beans, chick peas.	Shelling beans is an essential skill. Have the kids do it when they are just sitting around earlier in the day or the day before. (See Minty Peas with Butter on p. 117)
snow peas, pea pods	Very flat pea pods with underdeveloped seeds.	These are cooked and eaten pod and all. Do cut or pinch off the stem. A Big Green Salad (p. 8), Green Rice (p. 18), Pea Shoot Stir Fry (p. 43), Blanched Kohlrabi Marinated in Oil (p. 40), Artichoke Stems, Parmesan & Grains Salad (p. 48)	If the raw flavor has an unpleasant after taste, treat like green beans (see above) for crudité/veggie tray.